You

Did

That

on Purpose

_____

YOU
DID
THAT
ON PURPOSE

Understanding and Changing

Children's Aggression

Cynthia Hudley

Yale University Press
New Haven & London

Set in Minion Roman type by Keystone Typesetting, Inc., Orwigsburg, Pennsylvania.
Printed in the United States of America by Thomson-Shore, Inc., Dexter, Michigan.

Library of Congress Cataloging-in-Publication Data
Hudley, Cynthia.
You did that on purpose : understanding and changing children's aggression /
Cynthia Hudley.
p. cm.
Includes bibliographical references and index.
ISBN 978-0-300-11085-2 (alk. paper)
1. Aggressiveness in children. I. Title.
BF723.A35H83 2008
155.4'1247—dc22

2008003715

A catalogue record for this book is available from the British Library.

The paper in this book meets the guidelines for permanence and durability of the
Committee on Production Guidelines for Book Longevity of the Council on Library
Resources.

10 9 8 7 6 5 4 3 2 1

This volume is dedicated to:

my mother, Cynthia Duke Cox Hudley,
an authentic phenomenal woman,
without whom I could never have achieved all that I have

my husband, James Robert Hodge Cook,
whose love, support, and patience have lifted me up
throughout this task

Contents

Preface

This book derives from my enduring interest in children who have what I once thought of as inexplicably aggressive responses in social situations with other children. This interest emerged during my first years, if not weeks, as a teacher in a middle school, referred to euphemistically as an "opportunity school," for children who were having difficulty in the regular classroom. Scenes of indignation or outrage were an almost daily occurrence in our small learning community, and I, a novice teacher, struggled to make sense of what these children were doing to one another to arouse such heated aggression. My more experienced colleagues tended to chalk up the intense emoting to hormones. However, we could reliably expect any one of a relatively small, specific group of mostly boys to exhibit such disruptive behavior with some frequency.

In the midst of an organized activity, whether it was a quiet, sustained reading period or a lively, cooperative project, one of these young people would invariably lash out at a peer. One of the staff would dutifully pull the child aside and ask what brought on the aggressive, unhappy behavior. Just as dutifully, the child would reply, "He [or she] was 'looking at me funny, like they were making fun of me.'" Or perhaps, "I saw her [or him] look over at me and then start whispering, and I know they were talking bad about me." Or even, "Somebody bumped my desk [or book, or shoe]. And I know it must have been him [or her]." As the conversation progressed, I would invariably hear such things as "I just know it was them; I can tell." And if the misbehavior was far enough beyond the pale to warrant a punishment like lunch detention, yard pickup duty or some other unattractive task, the child would invariably reply, "See! He (or she) was trying to get me in trouble." No logic could convince the child that the response was not appropriate.

The behavior did not bother just the staff. Since peers also found the aggressive children particularly unattractive companions, the aggressive children wound up spending most of their time with others like them. Noticing that some children were social misfits in an opportunity school suggested to me that the behaviors that landed them in a social wasteland were a sign of far more than raging hormones. But I was young, and there was a lot to learn in a challenging environment, and somehow we all managed to get along enough of the time to engage academically. I considered it a success that most of my students learned well and moved back into the regular school population; the social anomalies would have to take care of themselves.

I never forgot the experience or the behaviors that I encountered working in that setting. Perhaps in that small, special school, there were disproportionate numbers of children who displayed such behaviors, and they were more salient. In any case, I traversed a professional career lasting more than a decade in a variety of roles in a variety of secondary schools. Through it all, the memories of those unaccountably aggressive, affronted children stayed with me. Imagine my surprise when I decided to go back to graduate school and found that my students of long ago had recently emerged in the research literature.

This fortuitous timing shaped the first decade of my academic career and resulted in a program of intervention research to address that disruptive and once baffling behavior. As much as the behavior distracted and challenged me as a novice teacher, I came to understand that it was far more debilitating for the aggressive students themselves. They live in a world where almost any negative event is counted a personal insult that must be met with immediate, direct retaliation. They have few friendships and many days of detention. They go through their days with a firm belief that others mean them harm and with little patience for any other explanation for events. Although I know that the world is not as safe a place as it should be for all children, some children see intentional insult where none exists and persistently refuse to distinguish between friend and foe. If the only social strategy one has is retaliation, the entire playground becomes the enemy. I hope that my efforts can make the playground a little friendlier for these children.

I could not possibly have made my way this far on my own, and I will be eternally grateful to all of those who encouraged, guided, and supported me along the way. These include my graduate school mentor and friend, Sandra Graham, who was especially helpful in getting me started down this path. I am also grateful for a cadre of smart, diligent graduate students, including Marlena Botts, David Wakefield, Brenda Britsch, Tara Knight, Su-je Cho, Candace Kelly, Whitney Scott, Kimberly White-Smith, Cam Vu, and Michelle Rosemond, whose hard work and long hours of travel allowed me to collect enough data to make sense of what I was doing. This intervention research would never have happened without the participation of the several school sites and after-school sites that opened their doors and allowed me to work with them, and I thank the staff, students, and parents for being a part of this process of development. The work has led me to interesting places with interesting people, and I am the better for it. I hope that I have given as much as I have received.

CHAPTER 1

A Look at Children's Aggression

Imagine that you are a fifth grader. You arrive at school in the morning, set your book bag on a bench, and run to the playground. You go back to the bench just a few minutes later. Your bag is lying under the bench in an inch of water. How did your bag end up on the ground? What are you going to do?

Meet Don, a fifth grader attending school in a working-class neighborhood, who described just such a situation to me. In a long, comfortable interview one day after school, Don told me about life on the school playground. To Don, school is a place where his fellow students are usually up to no good. He described a morning when a classmate "threw my bag on the ground." His teacher was strict about requiring students to come prepared for work, and anyone without school supplies lost privileges for the day. According to Don, when he left his bag on the bench, a classmate opened it and went through the contents in search of supplies for class. When the classmate could not find any notebook paper in Don's book bag that day, "he just threw it down under the lunch benches."

As we talked on, however, it became clear that Don had not seen anyone open his bag, nor could he even be sure that anything was missing from it. In fact, he was nowhere near the bag when the alleged attempt to steal from him took place. He could not point to any evidence that his bag had been opened and rifled; he even volunteered that it was not open and that none of the contents were lying on the ground when he came back to the bench after getting a breakfast tray. Neither were there witnesses to an attempted theft. In fact, he was sure that no one had seen anything, but he was equally sure that his bag was on the ground because a classmate had thrown it there.

Don was unable to imagine that his book bag simply rolled off the bench, was accidentally knocked off, or never landed on the bench when he dropped it off and headed for the food line. He was absolutely certain that a peer, in a very deliberate fashion, had wronged him by opening his book bag and then throwing it on the ground. I brought up several other kinds of information that suggested that he might be mistaken or that other explanations might be more reasonable. "What about the fact that no one saw it?" I asked. "Did you set it down really carefully, or were you in a hurry to get to the line? Were other people walking around in that area and maybe bumped into the bench?" None of the evidence that might lead to other, more benign explanations made any difference to Don. He knew what had happened, and my questions just confirmed for him that I "didn't know the people here" the way he did.

When I asked him to describe the best way to handle such a situation, Don first said that the best choice in this instance was to do nothing. "I just have to forget it because I can't prove who did it." Interestingly, he went right on to describe several things he had done later that day to a student who he was fairly sure had thrown the bag on the ground. Don's retaliation included taking the student's only pencil (causing the student to lose privileges that day), telling others not to play with this student at lunch, and telling another student that "he probably took some of your stuff too." Although he said that he had forgotten about the book-bag incident, Don's responses to specific questions made it clear that he had exacted retribution from the peer who had presumably done him harm.

When he "got even" later by taking the other student's pencil, Don retaliated with indirect aggression by causing that child to experience punishment from the teacher. When he told others not to play with this student, he used interpersonal relationships to harm the student. Such tactics, which psychologists call relational aggression, can include other things, like spreading hurtful rumors about someone or socially ostracizing someone from the peer group. Don's certainty that he had been intentionally harmed seems questionable; his targeting a specific peer seems even less likely to have been based on fact. Several things involving any number of people, including Don, may have caused that bag to end up on the ground. So Don's retaliatory aggression toward that particular child seems possibly to have been both unprovoked and inappropriate.

Don's decision to retaliate aggressively in an unclear situation is not unusual. My research experience with aggressive students over the years has shown that this pattern of aggression is more prevalent than one might think. Cory, a fourth grader, is another of many examples of students who see purposeful harm everywhere. Cory described a situation for me that resulted in another student "getting me in trouble." One day near the start of the school term, Cory was sitting at his desk when a classmate walking past bumped him with a backpack. According to Cory, this student "had to have seen me when he walked past my desk. He just doesn't like me." Yet when I asked him to tell me the things about that person or that situation which helped him decide that the person did this on purpose, Cory's response was "he doesn't like me, so he wants to get me in trouble. He does whatever he has to." I next asked Cory to tell me about some other problems with this student. Surprisingly, this supposed tormentor was new to both the school and the neighborhood, and the two boys had had little contact either in or out of the classroom. The bump itself was the evidence that the child "did not like" Cory. Cory calmly reported that "when he hit me with the backpack, I just did

what I had to do." Cory had jumped up and pushed the other child
hard enough to knock over a desk, which immediately got the teacher's attention. Cory wound up in the principal's office waiting for his
mother and an inevitable punishment.

Like Don, Cory assumed that someone acted toward him with
harmful intent, and he was equally impervious to information to the
contrary. I asked Cory about the size of the student's backpack, the
width of the aisle between desks, the times that he himself might
have bumped someone else. "Sometimes I might bump into a desk
on an accident," Cory agreed, because the desks in his class were
close together. Yet he could not apply that reasoning to the peer who
bumped him with the backpack. Cory could understand that acci-
dents happen, but only if his own actions were at fault. If he experienced a negative outcome from the actions of another, the action
must have been deliberate. Because he assumed that the other child
acted with hostile intentions, Cory believed that retaliation was appropriate, and direct physical aggression was his behavior of choice.

These are but two examples of students I have met in more than
a decade of work studying interpersonal aggression among elementary school students. I define aggression as behavior that is intended
to injure or harm another, and I have studied the links between
children's understanding of intentional behavior and their choices
for physically aggressive retaliation addressed to peers.

Like Don and Cory, a surprising number of students, boys in
particular, see intentional harm in ambiguous and even in apparently innocuous situations with their classmates and other students.
Most troubling, this perception of intentional harm is far too often
accompanied by some form of aggressive retaliation, whether it is
direct physical action, as with Cory, or indirect aggression, as with
Don. It is reasonable to expect anyone who is deliberately harmed to
respond to the perpetrator in some way, whether by withdrawing
from that person or by retaliating. So it is not surprising that those

who frequently see deliberate harm are more often aggressive than not, even when their behavior is provoked in questionable or ambiguous circumstances. Unfortunately, high rates of aggressive behavior, whatever their cause, can be a persistent characteristic of social behavior with lasting negative consequences.

The Stability of Aggression

Physically aggressive behavior in childhood has been convincingly linked to negative personal and social experiences, as well as a variety of dysfunctional life outcomes. The clearest, most persistent long-term finding has been the stability of aggression itself. Children, both boys and girls, who are highly aggressive in elementary school, are often highly aggressive in adolescence and adulthood (Broidy et al., 2003; Farrington, 1994; Huesmann et al., 2006). It is important to remember that not all highly aggressive children are violent as they grow older, but such children are certainly overrepresented in the population of violent adolescents and adults. The seventeen-year-old who carries a weapon, commits crimes, and physically threatens or assaults others was, more often than not, a nine-year-old who was often suspended for fighting on the playground. This continuity seems to hold true for girls as well, although the links between early and later behavior may not be as strong as they are for boys. Much has been written in recent years about girls' aggression, but the discussion is mainly about psychological bullying, cliques, and social relationships (for example, *Odd Girl Out* by Rachel Simmons). However, direct physical aggression in girls has reached unprecedented levels of public awareness (Associated Press, 2007).

Several well-respected studies have followed children across decades and found striking similarities in the development of children who demonstrate high levels of early aggressive behavior. In an early study (begun in 1961 in Britain), boys rated by teachers as highly aggressive at age twelve were most likely by age eighteen to fight often in public and with groups of other men. At age thirty-two, now adult, they also far more frequently admitted physically assaulting a spouse or female companion (Farrington, 1994). Perhaps the most notable American study from the same time period was begun in 1960 in Columbia County, New York, with a multiethnic sample of both boys and girls (Lefkowitz et al., 1977). Children aged eight who were rated by their peers as highly aggressive reported high rates of aggression themselves at age eighteen. By age thirty these individuals reported high rates of physical aggression toward spouses and children. Most troubling, the children who were highly aggressive at age eight were likely at age thirty to themselves have highly aggressive children (Huesmann et al., 1984).

A more recent project, the Carolina Longitudinal Study (Cairns & Cairns, 1994), was designed to investigate the experiences of girls and boys growing up at the start of the 1990s. A general multiethnic group of elementary and middle school children were followed for more than ten years. The study also identified a subgroup of the boys and girls considered most aggressive for very close monitoring. For these participants, aggression was again a consistent behavior over time. Participants with high teacher ratings of direct, confrontational aggression in elementary school continued to receive high teacher ratings for aggressive behavior through their high school career. The relatively constant level of aggressive behavior was true for both girls and boys. However, girls more often added the techniques like Don's that I earlier described as relational aggression. Starting in the middle elementary years, girls' aggressive behavior (and many boys' as well) typically expanded to include gossip, social exclusion, and psychological bullying.

The consistency in teacher ratings across eight years is especially noteworthy because each student attended a new classroom with a different teacher each year. These were not, then, the reports of a single person who might somehow have been biased by reputation or circumstance. Rather, individual perceptions of aggressive behavior for each child were distributed broadly across multiple schools and many teachers. In addition, the research team conducted behavioral observations for their subsample of highly aggressive children and a comparison group of average children. Again they found that children rated aggressive by teachers consistently got into more conflicts over time than did average children. These aggressive children were also more likely to use hurtful strategies, both physical and indirect, and were less likely to make amends to maintain a relationship after an aggressive encounter.

A recent study that followed a relatively smaller group of boys throughout the 1990s also found that aggression was a persistent behavior, even if it was measured as early as first grade (Schaeffer et al., 2003). The researchers used teacher observations to evaluate boys' behavior no less than annually until the seventh grade. Follow-up interviews were conducted via telephone when participants were in their early twenties to find how they were faring as they entered adulthood. Some boys remained stable in their nonaggressive behavior throughout the duration of the study and were doing well as they entered adulthood. Other boys who had been either moderately or highly aggressive in elementary school were still displaying aggression, and a sizeable proportion (as many as three-quarters of the high aggressive group) were not faring well. Finally, this study reported on a group of boys who were nonaggressive in early childhood but developed aggressive behavior by mid-elementary school and continued that behavior through adolescence and early adulthood; they, too, were not faring as well as their nonaggressive peers. The study did not find the reverse pattern. There were no boys whose aggression in early childhood declined significantly across time; however, the number of participants may have been too small to detect this kind of change, which has been found in other studies.

These well-known studies show that forms of behavior may change, but comparative levels of aggressive behavior measured in middle childhood tend to remain stable across time. Over the past twenty-five years, some research has suggested that stability in levels of aggression approximates the stability in measures of intelligence over the school years (Olweus, 1979). Although others have found that the stability of aggression depends on the length of time between two measurements of behavior and the ways behavior is measured (e.g., Cairns et al., 1989), there is a consensus that aggression is a relatively stable behavior across childhood and adolescence. This is true for both boys and girls (Moffitt et al., 2001).

Although high levels of physical aggression are less frequent in girls, when it does occur, girls can be more hostile and hurtful than many boys (Broidy et al., 2003; Cairns & Cairns, 1994). One interview from the Carolina study will illustrate this point. Donna, a tenth grader who was not socially disadvantaged, described a conflict in which a peer, Linda, slapped her. Donna responded by beating Linda until she "had a black eye" and "was bleeding all over" (Cairns & Cairns, 1994: 46). Donna felt unable to walk away after being slapped for fear of losing face in front of her friends. This example is all the more chilling when we remember that for some children, both boys and girls, early physical aggression establishes a pattern that persists throughout life.

Consequences of Aggressive Behavior in Childhood

The long-term stability of overt aggressive behavior is even more troubling because aggression carries a host of other negative developmental consequences, including delinquency and criminality, peer rejection, poor school adjustment, and mental health concerns. Thus, the aggressive child may not only persist in the negative behavior but also experience other life problems that similarly persist and accumulate over time, with enduring negative consequences in later life. Although much of this evidence is drawn from studies with boys only, aggression is a long-term problem for girls as well. Unfortunately, the rates of overt aggression among girls are growing faster than for boys. Recent evidence suggests that observed rates of direct physical aggression among adolescent girls are now more similar to those for adolescent boys than has ever been true before (Connor, 2002).

Peer rejection. In my research, I allow classmates to assess one another as a means to gauge each child's relative standing in the peer group. Students, using a secret ballot format similar to that used for a write-in candidate in an election, create a list of the classmates they like most and those they like least. They also list students in their class who display overt aggressive behavior. These methods made it very clear that both Don and Cory, who participated in one of my projects, were viewed quite negatively by their classmates.

Don was listed as liked most only once, yet twenty-five of his thirty-one classmates listed him as someone they liked least. Further, every single one of Don's thirty-one classmates listed him in response to at least one of three questions that described aggressive behavior, including fighting, having an explosive temper, and disrupting classroom activities. Don received a total of forty-nine nominations combined across these three questions; in fact, he received the most nominations for aggressive behavior in his entire school. Similarly, Cory was listed as liked least by seventeen of his twenty-seven classmates, and only two children listed him as liked most. Cory was listed in response to at least one question about aggression by twenty-one of twenty-seven students in his fourth-grade class. He received a total of thirty-seven nominations for aggression, the highest for any fourth grader at his school. Research over the years has reported similar results (Bierman, 2004).

Children in elementary school who engage in high rates of overt aggression are often rejected by their peers. Thus aggression, a relatively stable problem behavior, often (though not always) occurs with peer rejection, leading to adjustment outcomes that are quite problematic. The combination of aggression and rejection seems to occur most often among children in elementary school who show the greatest amounts of aggression, as was true for Don and Cory.

An important caveat, however, is that not all aggressive children are rejected by their peers. The elementary school children who are most likely to be rejected are both inappropriate in their aggression and socially incompetent. They tend to respond or retaliate aggressively at times when peers find the behavior unwarranted and in violation of the social norms of the peer group. In contrast, children who are perceived by peers either to be popular (Rose, Swenson & Waller, 2004) or to stand up for themselves when bullied or challenged are typically seen as socially skillful and are not rejected by other children. In fact, for popular children, particularly in adolescence, certain forms of aggression (e.g., verbal, indirect) and even bullying, when directed toward youth of lower social status, can enhance their standing in the eyes of peers.

Those children who display socially penalized, retaliatory aggression like Don's and Cory's are the ones most likely to be rejected (Bierman, 2004). As troubling as the stability of aggressive behavior might be, the combination of aggression and rejection is especially likely to lead to subsequent maladjustment. Highly aggressive, socially incompetent, and rejected children far too often experience difficulties with personal and social adjustment not just on elementary school playgrounds but also well into adolescence and adulthood.

Several studies have followed rejected elementary school children and found that aggressive-rejected children continue to be the most aggressive and least well adjusted of all groups of children (Haselager et al., 2002; Ialongo, Vaden-Kiernan & Kellam, 1998). One study, begun when children entered elementary school (Haselager et al., 2002), included reports from multiple sources (parents, teachers, and self). Findings made clear that children who were both aggressive and rejected in elementary school experienced significantly higher rates of self-reported depression and, like Don and Cory, far lower rates of peer-rated friendship compared to average-status children. As well, children who were aggressive but not rejected had some social difficulties but reported dramatically lower symptoms of depression relative to the aggressive-rejected group. Similar results have also been found with adolescents (Coie et al., 1995).

Some developmental theorists have proposed mechanisms to explain why the combination of early aggressiveness and peer rejection so strongly bends development toward social and emotional maladjustment. Psychologists working in mental health clinics were the first to describe emotional and behavioral maladjustment in ways that took environmental influences into account (Albee, 1982). These new models of behavior, called ecological models, proposed that stressors present in one's social context could serve as powerful sources of psychological and behavioral disorder. In such a social-contextual framework, peer rejection and social isolation represent significant sources of stress for aggressive children, leading to increased levels of aggression.

This social-contextual or ecological explanation sounds somewhat similar to a more recent and more elaborated theory proposed by those who study children's development. Aggressive-rejected children are more often the targets of peer aggression than are other children and are the least likely to be included in peer activities, largely because of their reputations for aggressive and disruptive behavior (Bierman, 2004). Thus, children with a reputation for being aggressive evoke a markedly hostile peer environment in which they must interact, in an escalating cycle of aggression, rejection, and retaliation. The stress of such a hostile social environment may help explain the psychological distress that many aggressive-rejected children and youths experience. This escalating cycle, or model of reputational bias (Hymel, Wagner & Butler, 1990), has been explored as an explanation for the persistence of children's aggressive behavior.

The connection between aggressive-rejected status in childhood and maladaptive outcomes later in life may also be related to an inability to connect with a socially competent peer group. Aggressive children face restricted interpersonal options as a function of their reputation for aggression and rejection. Therefore they may find themselves part of a deviant peer group composed of other children with similar behaviors (Barnow, Lucht & Freyberger, 2005; Patterson, Reid & Dishion, 1992). Without opportunities for positive peer interactions, these children fail to develop the social competence that would allow them to succeed in more normative peer groups. Instead, these youths continue in groups that, over time, develop into antisocial cliques that reinforce aggression, delinquency, and other behaviors that further distance them from opportunities to interact with better adjusted peers (Cairns et al., 1988). In this cycle, aggression and peer rejection combine to accelerate the distance between successful and maladaptive development. This movement of physically aggressive rejected children away from their better adjusted peers is most marked for elementary school girls (Crick, 1997).

It is more typical for initial displays of aggressive behavior to cause a child to be rejected by other children than for initial experiences of rejection to lead a child to become highly aggressive. As time goes on, however, rejected status also encourages aggressive behavior. For Don and Cory, an early penchant for aggressive, disruptive behavior is likely to have led to the remarkably high levels of negative nominations they received, rather than the reverse.

Early laboratory research that brought together groups of unacquainted boys (Coie & Kupersmidt, 1983) demonstrated that aggressive behavior is likely to come before peer rejection. Boys were first categorized as rejected, popular, or average by using ratings from their elementary school classmates. Then one rejected boy was put into a group of five average or popular boys from five different schools for weekly play sessions. Within four weeks, the rejected boy was almost always rejected by this new group of playmates. More recent studies of both boys and girls in natural interactions with peers also find that aggressive behavior seems to precede rejection, from preschool (Arnold et al., 1999) to late adolescence (Eronen & Nurmi, 2001).

Even large studies that use teacher and parent ratings of aggression and follow children over several years have found that peer rejection often, but not always, predicts later aggression (Kupersmidt & DeRosier, 2004; Laird et al., 2001). The relationship between aggression and rejection depends on who is rating the child's behavior (teachers, parents, self) and the gender of the child. For example, peer rejection in elementary school predicts teacher ratings of aggression for boys and parent ratings of aggression for girls in adolescence (Ialongo, Vaden-Kiernan & Kellam, 1998).

Although findings that early aggressive behavior leads to peer rejection are relatively consistent for boys, the findings are less consistent for girls. If some studies find that rejection predicts adolescent aggression only as reported by parents (Ialongo et al., 1998) or by the girls themselves, other research suggests that early aggression predicts subsequent rejection equally for girls (Crick, 1997; Kupersmidt & DeRosier, 2004). Finally, some findings suggest that for girls, early rejection may predict more strongly that the individual will experience internalizing problems (e.g., depressive symptoms) rather than problems with aggression (Ialongo, Vaden-Kiernan & Kellam, 1998). In sum, although the data are more mixed for girls, it is safe to say that rejection is quite problematic for girls as well as for boys and that it has some impact on the subsequent development of aggressive and violent behavior in both sexes.

Delinquency and criminality. A robust consequence of early aggressive behavior is a heightened probability of criminal activity later in life. Several measures of childhood aggression (primarily in boys) have been repeatedly linked to adolescent delinquency and adult criminality, and that linkage is strengthened for children who are both aggressive and rejected by their peers. Whether boys' behavior is judged by themselves, teachers, peers, or clinicians or in institutional records, high levels of earlier aggression have been linked in a variety of studies to later arrest, adjudication, and/or incarceration within the juvenile and criminal justice systems for many of these youths (Broidy et al., 2003; Conner, 2002).

Early research that followed the same children over time to understand the relationship between aggression and later-life outcomes found that teacher ratings of aggression for children aged ten and thirteen could predict whether and how often boys might be arrested by age twenty-six. In particular, two of three boys with the highest ratings of aggression at age ten had been arrested at least once by age twenty-six, and nearly half (43 percent) had been arrested at least four times. In comparison, only 15 percent of boys with the lowest aggression ratings at age ten had been arrested at all, and none had been arrested more than once (Stattin & Magnusson, 1989). More recent studies have similarly found that early aggression is strongly related to violent criminality for boys later in life. Research that followed boys living in high-crime urban areas found that men convicted of a violent crime in young adulthood (age thirty and under) were more than three times as likely to have been rated by teachers and parents as highly aggressive in childhood or early adolescence than a comparison group of men who were not convicted of such crimes (Loeber et al., 2005). Even involvement in property crimes has been clearly linked to physical aggression measured as early as kindergarten (Haapasalo & Tremblay, 1994; Tremblay et al., 1994).

Findings also suggest that aggression may lead to adult criminality for girls. One early study demonstrated that aggression measured in early adolescence was highly predictive of criminality by age twenty-six. Seventy percent of girls with the highest ratings of aggression at age thirteen had been arrested at least once by age twenty-six, but not a single girl with the lowest ratings had been arrested (Stattin & Magnusson, 1989). Longitudinal data to link early aggression to later criminality among girls are sorely lacking, however (Krohn et al., 2001). What is clear is that arrests for violent delinquency are increasing more rapidly among girls than among boys (Kempf-Leonard, Chesney-Lind & Hawkins, 2001), and the proportion of females in the population of violent delinquents has been on the rise since 1987. Girls now represent up to one-third of the youths arrested for serious and violent crimes in some urban communities (Snyder & Sickmund, 1999). Arrest rates for juveniles (ages ten–seventeen), though lower now than in 1995, increased in some categories much more rapidly for females than for males from 1980 to 2004. Aggravated assault (93 percent versus 11 percent for females and males, respectively) and weapons violations (160 percent versus 22 percent) are two categories related to aggressive behavior that have shown marked increases for females (Snyder, 2006). Clearly, a link between aggression and delinquency among girls merits particular attention if we want to understand the developmental trajectories that lead to such problematic outcomes.

Compared to average children, then, children who were highly aggressive in elementary school seem more prone to commit crimes in adolescence and adulthood, whether they are arrested or not. Aggression often predicts later criminality whether the reports on crimes committed come from the youths themselves, from their parents and teachers, or from the justice system. This relationship holds true to some extent for both boys and girls. In addition, the crimes are more often crimes of violence against persons rather than property crimes; assault and battery are more common offenses in the group rated highly aggressive than among their nonaggressive peers. Evidence points to the conclusion that high levels of aggression in childhood can be an indicator, though sometimes an imperfect one, of violent delinquency and criminality later in life.

School adjustment and achievement. High levels of aggression are linked to poor school adjustment and achievement across time and across cultures. Studies with students from elementary school through adolescence typically find that aggressive students tend to be poorly adjusted as they progress through school and through life. Teacher and peer ratings of both American (Cairns, Cairns & Neckerman, 1989) and Chinese students (Chen, Rubin & Li, 1997) demonstrate that aggressive students are perceived as generally less academically successful, more behaviorally disruptive, and less motivated in class (e.g., off task, not doing homework) in comparison to their nonaggressive peers.

Aggressive behavior sometimes more effectively predicts poor academic functioning rather than the reverse (see Hinshaw, 1992, for a review of these studies). For example, studies with American (Masten et al., 1995) and with Chinese (Chen, Rubin & Li, et el., 1997) youth have found that aggression in earlier grades predicts poor school achievement in later grades, but earlier achievement difficulties did not predict later aggression. High levels of aggression in elementary school have negative effects on educational and career attainment that can persist even into mid-adulthood (Dubow et al., 2006). Further, both aggression and rejection measured in elementary school (Risi, Gerhardstein & Kistner, 2003) and middle school (French & Conrad, 2001) and even measured as early as first grade (Ensminger & Slusarcick, 1992) predict educational difficulties (low achievement, poor adjustment) and early high-school dropout.

Academic poor performance can, however, intensify aggressive behavior (Arnold, 1997; Miles & Stipek, 2006). Aggression in the middle elementary grades has been specifically related to poor literacy skills, including word decoding and reading comprehension, and these skill limitations predict later aggressive behavior. The mechanisms that seem to explain the relationships between aggression and academic achievement in elementary school are inattentiveness and disciplinary problems. In middle childhood, boys, in particular those who are often off task and inattentive, whether owing to poor academic skills (Arnold, 1997; Miles & Stipek, 2006) or conduct problems (Masten et al., 1995), are presumably more likely to be disciplined by teachers than are other students. When a teacher's discipline takes the form of removal either from classroom instruction (e.g., time out) or from the classroom itself (e.g., sent to the principal's office), it is not surprising that academic progress is undermined.

Clearly, the link between aggression and school achievement is student behavior. This very brief review of a large research literature makes the case that children who are highly aggressive display dysfunction not only in social behavior but also in academic behavior and peer relationships, no matter whether poor academic skills lead to childhood aggression or aggressive behavior impedes academic development. Highly aggressive elementary school children tend to be rejected by peers and to display low motivation, inattentiveness, and frequent off-task and disruptive behavior. In middle school, peer ratings of social rejection and aggressive behavior continue to be related to poor academic motivation and teacher perceptions of poor motivation, poor self-control (e.g., highly impulsive or noncompliant behavior), and poor achievement. By middle school, teachers' perceptions of motivation in individual students relate positively to both academic attainment (i.e., grade point average) and a teacher's preference for working with that student (Wentzel & Asher, 1995).

Poor teacher and peer relations may contribute to aggressive students' poor adjustment and achievement above and beyond the effects of their own inappropriate behavior. We have seen that academic achievement is compromised by inappropriate classroom behaviors such as inattentiveness, disruptiveness, and poor motivation. These behaviors reduce children's ability not only to benefit from classroom instruction but also to establish positive relations with both teachers and peers. Peer relations may be especially significant in cooperative learning activities, where social skills may be necessary to master an assignment. Similarly, inappropriate behavior seems to be a disincentive for a teacher to work independently with a particular student.

Findings of gender differences in the relation between aggression and academic competence are inconsistent. Some studies find that overtly aggressive girls in particular may be more at risk for school failure and dropout in adolescence than are nonaggressive girls (Walker et al., 1998). Some findings of gender difference suggest that boys' aggression has significant effects on academic adjustment, but girls' academic adjustment is affected by more general oppositional behavior (Bierman et al., 2004). Some studies find no gender differences at all in the impact of overt aggression on school adjustment (Cairns et al., 1989; Wentzel & Asher, 1995). These conflicting results have been generated by studies done on a range of populations (urban, rural, ethnic minority, white, early- and middle-childhood, adolescent, disadvantaged, middle-income). Therefore, the relationship between aggressive behavior and difficulties in school may be influenced by a wide range of individual difference and contextual variables, including gender. Nevertheless, the connection between childhood aggression and poor academic outcome has been well established in the research literature for both boys and girls across a broad range of ages and sociocultural contexts.

Prevention and Intervention

The foregoing brief, selective review of the literature touched on peer rejection, delinquency, and school achievement, three consequences of perhaps greatest concern to parents, educators, and policymakers. However, a variety of equally compelling findings must be left unaddressed. For example, childhood aggression has been linked to serious life problems in adulthood, including employment difficulties, mental and emotional distress (depression, anxiety), and substance abuse (i.e., alcohol and drugs; Rutter, Giller & Hagell, 1998). An exhaustive review of life-span consequences of childhood aggression is beyond the scope of this book. Nevertheless, this introductory review leaves little doubt about the significance of the problem of aggression in childhood.

The major thesis of this book is that some children are prone to a particular style of attending to, thinking about, and reacting to social information when they are with their peers. This style of social information processing leads children to presume that any negative outcome with a peer is the result of intentionally harmful behavior. While anyone who is deliberately harmed is likely to at least consider some kind of retaliation, children who see harmful intent where it does not exist are especially prone to excessive and inappropriate physical retaliation.

The following chapters will address that thesis by discussing some of the causes, consequences, and strategies for remediation of childhood aggression. I will begin by describing the tendency to overestimate intentional harm, how this tendency facilitates children's aggressive behavior, and the negative consequences from the peer group that are elicited by the aggression that results from this biased way of thinking. I will then discuss what can be done to help children overcome this particular style of social reasoning by describing the core of my research for the past decade. That program of research has been the development, assessment, and field testing of an intervention for elementary school students that is designed specifically to address aggressive behavior that results from children's biased thinking.

In the final chapters of the book I will examine selected factors that are associated with interpersonal aggression in children along with several additional evidence-based interventions that have successfully reduced childhood aggression. Aggression is a behavior that is subject to multiple determinants, and no single intervention should be considered a panacea. Rather, I assert that changing children's patterns of social reasoning is only one piece of what must be a comprehensive set of strategies to reduce childhood aggression. Separate chapters will thus deal with schools, parental socialization, and broad social policies.

In discussing school factors relevant to the development and display of childhood aggression, I will examine school policies and training for school staff, including pre-service teachers. The goal is to explore the ways schools can promote peaceful campuses and model peaceful interactions among the adults, between the adults and the children, *and* among the children. Suggestions for whole school strategies will include a curricular emphasis on nonviolence, awards for "peaceful" students, and an examination of the school discipline policies and practices to ensure that adults model nonviolence in their interactions with students. In addition to specific strategies, the book will provide a selective review of whole school programs that have been rigorously evaluated in elementary schools.

The discussion then moves beyond schools to consider family socialization practices. For example, research on gender socialization suggests why boys are particularly prone to aggression and why this trend may be increasing in girls. I will also present what we know about parent-child interactions and the development of aggression. For example, certain styles of discipline early in life are related to higher levels of aggression in later childhood. Parental monitoring of children's free time and friendships has a direct bearing on children's antisocial behavior. A committed, nurturing father can be a powerful force in raising socially competent, nonaggressive children. Conversely, the experience of poverty can be an equally powerful force in the development of antisocial behavior in children. I will next describe research-based techniques that can be of help to parents who want to rear socially competent children. Parents will be encouraged to model peaceful interactions with their peers and their children, to discuss and encourage peaceful solutions to problems, to monitor television viewing and other recreational activities, and to monitor their children's friends and their children's friends' behavior.

The book will conclude with a brief discussion of public policy that permits all children to experience successful developmental outcomes rather than turning to antisocial behavior. *You Did That on Purpose* is not intended as a treatise on the appropriate direction of social policy for this country; however, I will explore what we know about the basic requirements for successful behavioral development in childhood. Social policies and practices that have an impact on children's healthy development include the media glorification of aggression and violence, the juvenile justice system's repudiation of rehabilitation, and the environment and guidance provided in every community for all of its children.

In sum, the chapters that follow will provide compelling theory and research on the causes and consequences of childhood aggression as well as practical suggestions for intervention to reduce children's peer-directed aggression. The goal is to introduce a novel and effective intervention program for reducing childhood aggression along with the necessary support in schools, families, and communities to ensure healthy social, emotional, and intellectual development in childhood and beyond.

CHAPTER 2

Understanding Intent
One Source of Childhood Aggression

Think for a moment of a typical elementary school playground, where children routinely spend time waiting in line to eat, to take a turn in a game, and to engage in any number of other activities. If one of those children is bumped hard from behind by a peer while standing in line, what do you think will happen next? The child who has been bumped has a range of possible responses, some aggressive, some not. In this chapter I want to describe how children's thinking about the world around them has been linked with an increased inclination to use aggressive behavior when interacting with other children. If we want to predict whether the child in our example will turn around and throw a punch at the peer's head or look back to find out what is going on, one of the best indicators is to understand how that child thinks about and interprets the behavior of other children.

Don and Cory, whose aggressive behavior was discussed earlier, were certain that they had experienced intentional harm from peers. The two boys used that belief to justify the aggression, both direct and indirect, that they displayed toward peers in return. In fact, those of us who study child development and aggression have examined beliefs about intentions for more than twenty years. Research with children over a long period of time has made it clear that when children assume that others mean them intentional harm, such presumptions can contribute directly and powerfully to the display of angry aggressive behavior.

It is reasonable to expect a response of some kind from anyone who believes that he or she has been intentionally harmed. Unfortunately, a child's reasoning about the social world can lead to the perception of intentional harm where none exists. Too many children feel justified in using unnecessary aggressive retaliation precisely because they incorrectly see deliberate harm in a peer's behavior. Some children's automatic thinking processes support high levels of aggressive behavior and leave them vulnerable to negative lifetime consequences that may result from such behavior.

Attributions of Intent

More than two decades ago, research with aggressive children identified a pattern of thinking that overestimates harmful intent in others. This pattern was labeled hostile attributional bias (Dodge, 1980; Nasby, Hayden & DePaulo, 1980). In essence, an attribution answers the "why" question: "Why did you bump into me?" "Why did you knock my books on the floor?" When a person assigns a cause to the behavior of others, an attribution has been made (Weiner, 1986). Attributions are a normal part of social interaction and have been studied in both children and adults for half a century (Weiner, 1992). Everyone makes attributions while interacting with others because people often try to understand the reasons why a particular outcome occurs in a variety of social situations. Although we do not make attributions for the causes of behavior in every single situation, everyone is likely to look for causes when a social interchange results in a negative outcome (e.g., my books end up in the floor).

Psychological theories that are designed to explain the reasoning behind particular attributions describe a set of common beliefs and assumptions that guide our thinking about the causes of behavior

(Weiner, 1992). To understand attributions that may lead to aggression, perceptions of personal control are one key and beliefs about intent are another. If you knock my books off of my desk, were the circumstances beyond your personal control? Is the classroom overcrowded because additional desks were brought in, so students can no longer walk around without bumping into desks? Or did you stuff your own backpack so full that it hangs down too low to fit through the rows between desks? Or did you purposefully walk by my desk just so you could bump it?

To make an attribution of hostile intent, the perceiver must believe that the outcome was not the result of environmental conditions, that the other person was in control of the behavior that caused the negative outcome, and that the other person intended the outcome to happen. Only the third of our proposed explanations for the desk bump scenario fits the requirements for an attribution of hostile intent. In the first explanation, clearly you are not in control of the overcrowded conditions. In the second possible explanation, although your backpack was so full that it was too big to navigate through the classroom, there was no intent to use the backpack to knock books off the desks. The average child or adult, given either of these two explanations, would attribute the scenario to accidental causes. However, a child like Cory or Don, with a hostile attributional bias, would very likely attribute the scenario to hostile intentions on the part of the offending peer, irrespective of the circumstances. In discussing an actual situation with Cory that was quite similar to this classroom scenario, he indeed saw the peer's offense exactly as we would predict for a child with a hostile attributional bias.

How Bias Works with Memory

A great deal of research has explored the kind of thinking that defines hostile attributional bias. For one thing, children like Don and Cory seem to misjudge the hostility of peers because they respond quickly, without thinking about the social situation. One very early study, using a board game format, demonstrated this apparent inattentiveness to the social messages available in the behavior of others. Researchers developed a detective game that children played to uncover the causes of negative outcomes in several hypothetical scenarios. The participants, all boys, had to select written clue cards in order to make decisions about various characters in the scenarios. Those children who displayed attributional bias made decisions about characters' intentions and behaviors using fewer "clues" than average children used (Dodge and Newman, 1981). Rather than using the social information contained in the clue cards, children with biases appeared to base their judgments on preexisting beliefs that peers would behave aggressively and with hostile intentions.

Early work also found that children with this kind of biased thinking were likely to rely on preexisting beliefs rather than thinking about what actually happened in a social situation. Children with this kind of bias who either heard stories read aloud or viewed videotapes were far more successful in "recalling" hostile information, even if it had not been present in the story (Dodge and Frame, 1982). They were also far less successful in recalling positive information that had been presented than were average children (Dodge and Tomlin, 1987).

This inattentiveness to available social information in children with an attributional bias is simply a distortion of the normative "mental shorthand" that we all use to navigate social encounters. Our minds would be overwhelmed if we had to attend to every individual piece of social information every time we interacted with another person. Instead, in social interactions, people usually use memories of past events in similar situations as guides in deciding how to behave in ways appropriate for the situation. These memories of past events are stored in structures that psychologists refer to as causal schemas and scripts (Kelley, 1973).

A causal schema is a mental picture, or map, of what we expect to happen in a given situation, how to behave appropriately in that situation, and what outcome we can expect from that behavior (Huesmann, 1998). This schema is composed of several scripts. Scripts help us organize and structure the particular social interactions that can get us successfully through the sequence of events that we expect in that situation. Initially, expectations of situations come from experiences that we build up early in life. These early experiences and expectations become the substance of schemas and scripts that we store in memory (Huesmann, 1998).

For instance, fast food restaurants rely on the fact that most customers have had enough experience in these particular kinds of businesses to develop a schema that allows them to transact business quickly (e.g., check the posted menu, place an order, pay, get a receipt with a pickup number, listen for the number, take the food). The process is sufficiently familiar that everyone, customers and staff alike, has a standard set of scripts to guide the interaction at each step in the transaction. As a result, veteran customers have very little need to monitor and evaluate the details of the entire situation to determine appropriate behavior in this setting, a strategy that would considerably slow down the social action.

As can be seen from the fast food example, mental schemas allow us to function in a world that would otherwise overwhelm us with information. Rather than attending to each and every social cue, we focus on whatever we think is important in a social setting and allow our schema to "fill in" the rest. In a fast food restaurant, all we have to recognize is that we are in a particular type of familiar establishment. We may not attend to the color on the servers' uniforms; we may not notice the noise level or the conversations of the people around us. Depending on our prior experiences and current needs, we may single out only certain information (e.g., price of the food, cleanliness of the establishment, speed of service). We then fill in the rest of the details for a successful transaction from a schema stored in our memory that describes a fast food restaurant.

While schemas help us to function in the social world without becoming overwhelmed by details, attributions are the immediate thinking processes that help us decide how to respond to specific social cues in an interaction. The two mental processes work together to determine the behavior that a person will display in any specific situation. An attributional bias, guided by a schema stored in memory, prompts us to focus on specific cues while ignoring many others and promotes a singular interpretation of those cues. Thus, schemas are memories, general templates, or pictures of social interactions; attributions are thought processes that interpret a single interaction.

Recall Don, who walked onto the playground with his book bag. He probably entered the playground with a schema that prepared him to expect a peer to act toward him with hostile intent. When he did in fact experience a negative outcome (his book bag landed in a puddle), his attributional bias caused him to interpret this particular outcome as the result of a peer's hostile intent. Rather than looking for causes in the immediate situation, he attended to social evidence that was foregrounded by his schema for peer interactions and then interpreted that evidence with a bias consistent with his schema. Don's only task was to identify the peer who had done a wrong to him. His attributional bias permitted no other interpretation, and his schema required little information from the actual sequence of events. His schema and attributional bias provided everything he needed to make sense of the situation.

Similarly, Cory's decision to physically retaliate against what was likely an accidental bump was guided by his patterns of thinking rather than the existing situation. Ha also probably possessed a schema that anticipated hostility from peers in school, and his attributional bias, similar to Don's, caused him to focus only on those cues that confirmed his expectations. Cory's schema undoubtedly comprised aggressive and accusatory scripts that guided his exchange with the offending peer and did little to defuse the situation.

How Memory and Attributional Bias Support Aggressive Behavior

In Don and Cory, we have compelling examples of how memory stores favoring aggression and biased attributions unite to produce highly aggressive behavior in children. In fact, attributional bias was originally identified in studies attempting to understand the causes for high levels of reactive aggression in some children. The earliest published study (Nasby, Hayden & DePaulo, 1980) included boys in middle childhood and adolescence who were receiving residential treatment for emotional disturbance, a serious condition that may include aggressive and violent behavior. Participants matched photographs of faces with emotion labels (e.g., hostility, sadness, anger, fear). Caseworkers also rated boys' aggressive behavior. For all participants, the higher the rating of aggressive behavior from caseworkers, the more frequently the boy also incorrectly identified photographs as showing hostility.

Another foundational study with a similar identification task extended these important findings to the general population of elementary school boys (Dodge, Murphy & Buchsbaum, 1984). Participants watched videotaped scenes of small groups of boys (just two or three) in situations that ended with a negative outcome (e.g., a push, lost homework). The dialogue was structured such that intent could be identified as either hostile ("I meant to push you"), accidental ("I fell into you because I tripped"), or helpful ("I pushed you to the side so you wouldn't step in the mud puddle"). In this study, all the children were quite accurate in identifying hostile intent in the videotapes. However, aggressive participants made far more errors than their less aggressive peers in identifying accidental and helpful intents. Aggressive participants' mistakes were largely attributions of hostile intent where none was presented.

The groundbreaking study examining attributional bias in the general population of elementary school boys used very different methods (Dodge, 1980). Researchers in this study gave boys a puzzle assembly task. During the task, boys had the opportunity to dismantle an unseen peer's puzzle after they were led to believe that this unseen person had dismantled the work they themselves were doing. Their impression of the unseen peer's intent was manipulated by using one of three audio recordings containing an explanation that indicated an accidental, hostile, or ambiguous intent. In deciding whether to break up the peer's puzzle, aggressive boys were equally aggressive in their behavior in the ambiguous and hostile intent situations and were relatively less aggressive in response to the accidental intent situation. Among nonaggressive boys, behavior was restrained in the ambiguous and accidental intent situations and relatively more aggressive in the hostile intent situation. Thus, while all boys changed their behavior according to their perception of the peer's intent, aggressive boys showed a particular tendency to presume hostile intent in an ambiguous situation. Only the aggressive boys appeared to make a hostile intent attribution and to retaliate in kind when they were unsure of the intent. Nonaggressive boys apparently presumed accidental intent and decided not to destroy the puzzle when they were unsure of the intent.

A similar study (Steinberg & Dodge, 1983) extended findings to both girls and boys using a block-building task. Participants worked in same-sex pairs to design and build a block tower to win a prize. However, the children were intentionally distracted before they finished building the tower. They returned to the task to discover that some blocks had fallen off and their tower was damaged. Later, each student was asked individually why she or he thought that had happened. Participants, both boys and girls, whose behavior had been rated aggressive by teachers were likely to attribute their misfortune to the hostile behavior of peers, whereas nonaggressive participants were much less likely to make such attributions.

Finally, a comparative study (Lochman & Dodge, 1994) was the first to explain the systematic range of differences in patterns of thinking, including attributions, for three groups of boys with greater or lesser behavior problems: (1) those clinically diagnosed as violently aggressive, (2) those rated aggressive by teachers but not referred for psychiatric evaluation, and (3) those rated by teachers as nonaggressive. Each participant individually watched videotaped scenes of child actors in conflicts with peers and was then asked to imagine that each scene had really happened to him. Scenes showed either overtly hostile intentions, positive intentions, or ambiguous intentions. Each child was asked to interpret the intentions of the peer. As with earlier studies, boys with a clinical diagnosis as violent were most likely to interpret peer intentions as hostile, regardless of the content of the videotaped scenes. Boys rated aggressive by teachers also displayed a hostile attributional bias but did not make as many errors as the clinically violent boys. Nonaggressive boys made few errors overall in their judgments of intent. This study was one of the first to compare boys across levels of aggressive behavior, and the results suggest that as aggressive behavior increases, attributional bias increases. Similarly, recent research comparing both boys and girls who are either highly aggressive or very withdrawn reveals a similar pattern. Boys and girls in elementary and middle school who are highly aggressive are more likely than their extremely withdrawn classmates to attribute hostile intentions to peers in ambiguous situations (Burgess et al., 2006).

These foundational studies represent the underpinnings of the wealth of research that has been conducted on how aggressive children, both boys and girls, think about the behavior of other children (for recent reviews see Gifford-Smith & Rabiner, 2004; Orobio de Castro et al., 2002). This body of literature presents evidence of a clear and compelling relationship between aggressive behavior and attributions of intent. Children who are highly aggressive are likely to perceive others around them as acting with hostile intent. They make mistakes when judging the intent of others, and they act on their mistaken attributions of hostile intent. Retaliation is not so surprising from one who believes he or she has been harmed intentionally. So high rates of aggressive behavior are predictable from anyone who sees others as behaving toward him or her with hostile intent most of the time. An attributional bias leads the perceiver to incorrectly see harm where none exists and thus evokes inappropriate responses that include high rates of aggressive behavior.

We also now understand that memories, in the form of cognitive schemas, work together with attributional bias in guiding aggressive behavior. Recall that schemas are products of our accumulated experiences, stored in memory. The unique socialization experiences from families and peers of some children seem to create aggressive schemas and scripts that differ in both quality and quantity from those that guide less aggressive children.

Researchers who study the relationship between an infant and its primary caretaker, usually a parent, talk about how well the child is attached, or emotionally connected, to the caretaker. This well-researched theory of family interaction in early life has long suggested that early experiences with a parent or other caretaker provide a child with an early and deeply ingrained schema of relationships (Crittenden & Ainsworth, 1989). Children who experience harsh treatment from caregivers early in life may come to understand all relationships as threatening and dangerous. Strong evidence indicates that children who experience early physical abuse display high rates of aggressive behavior in childhood and adulthood (Finzi et al., 2001). Similarly, even parenting that involves harsh, punitive discipline but does not reach the level of child abuse predicts increased levels of aggression as children enter adolescence (Knutson, DeGarmo & Reid, 2004). Once children perceive relationships as threatening, it is unsurprising that they respond with aggression whenever they experience negative outcomes in situations with peers. Relationship schemas may partially explain how early experiences of anger and abuse get translated into aggressive behavior in childhood and beyond.

Recent research with relatively younger children (Dodge et al., 2003) has explored how memories of peer experiences can also shape aggression. For young children who are aggressive, the memory of early rejection by peers changes the way these children think in later social encounters. The research team of K. Dodge and others followed children from kindergarten to grade 3 for three years, collecting responses to videotaped scenarios and teacher ratings of behavior each year. As initially aggressive children grew older, they were likely to be rejected by peers. These children, both boys and girls, became increasingly attentive to social cues that indicated hostility and increasingly likely to believe that aggression was a good solution for social problems. Such changes in children's thinking assured that they would act even more aggressively. The authors concluded that for aggressive children, memories of social rejection during early school years increase an existing attributional bias. Thus, initially aggressive children are caught in a negative cycle; as rejection increases, attributional bias increases, which in turn increases the likelihood of aggressive behavior.

By middle childhood, roughly ages seven to twelve, children with a reputation for being aggressive evoke a markedly more hostile social environment in which they must interact. Displays of angry aggression typically provoke peers to respond with heightened aggression and rejection (Hymel, Wagner & Butler, 1990). As a consequence, aggressive young children may enter school only to experience an escalating cycle of aggression, rejection, and retaliation in interactions with peers. My own research suggests that there may be a similar cycle with caretakers (Hudley & Graham, 1994). When asked to think about their school-age child's misbehavior (e.g., leaving the kitchen dirty, losing a school report), mothers of aggressive boys consistently attributed more deliberately negative intent to the child, reported feeling more anger and less sympathy, and rated harsher punishments more appropriate in comparison to mothers of nonaggressive boys. Thus, biases in cognition and aggressive relationship schemas established early in life may be further elaborated and consolidated by experiences with peers and parents.

As a result of life experiences, aggressive children have schemas that incorporate higher amounts and more serious kinds of aggressive behavior than do nonaggressive children. In addition, they simply have more aggressive schemas stored in memory. These schemas seem to have a powerful influence in the lives of aggressive children, who think about and elaborate aggressive schemas in fantasy play and daily activities. For instance, aggressive children pay particular attention to aggressive content in media like video games, movies, and music videos and seem to ignore less aggressive content. Research has also demonstrated that aggressive schemas are more readily available and accessible in aggressive children's thinking than they are in nonaggressive children (Graham & Hudley, 1994).

Using a practice called "priming" that is very often used in research with adults, a colleague, Sandra Graham, and I read aloud to groups of boys negative outcome stories that either reminded them of intentionally negative behavior (disobeying rules leads to losing a championship game) or reminded them of accidental behavior (going to the wrong playing field leads to losing the championship game). We then read a series of negative outcome stories in which the intent of the actors was unclear or ambiguous. We found that aggressive boys consistently labeled actions in these ambiguous stories as intentional and hostile, no matter what intent was portrayed in the initial stories. Nonaggressive boys saw intentional hostility in the ambiguous stories only if they had earlier heard stories that caused them to think about negative intent. From these results we concluded that only aggressive boys have schemas or memories of hostile intentions that remain constantly active and readily accessible in situations with negative outcomes. Based on past learning and experiences, these schemas become part of the way aggressive children make sense of their social world, even in situations in which the schemas and attributional biases that they trigger might not be appropriate.

A Research-Based Program of Behavior Change

The extensive findings on the reciprocal relationship between escalating aggression and changes in thinking patterns suggest an approach to changing aggressive behavior. Those of us who design interventions find that if the cycle can be interrupted in its early stages, the reciprocal relationship between thinking and behavior can work in a positive direction. Neither early experience nor childhood behavior represents unalterable destiny or permanently fixed schemas; a child's trajectory can be altered. Peer relations can be restored, attributional biases changed, and aggression forestalled or reduced.

Our understanding of the patterns of thinking that support children's aggression is well founded. Children whose stored memories or schemas are hostile and aggressive are relatively more likely than peers with fewer aggressive schemas to display biases in their decisions about the intentions of others. These patterns of hostile thinking directly support children's aggressive behavior. However, as the data giving rise to these conclusions were being collected, not many researchers were thinking about the possibility of changing behavior by changing children's patterns of thinking.

I began thinking about the appropriate application of research findings on children's thinking to intervention programs because theory and research clearly demonstrated that thinking about social situations can guide one's choice of social behavior. I concluded that changing children's attributions should change their behavior as well. My thinking culminated in a structured intervention program to reduce aggressive behavior during middle childhood that is based directly on the rich theoretical understanding of children's thinking that has been presented in this very brief review.

CHAPTER 3

The BrainPower Program
A Strategy for Changing Attributions

Before 1990, the research literature on child development was virtually silent on the application of our understanding of children's thinking patterns to the development of intervention programs to reduce children's aggression. However, in tandem with our growing understanding of children's thinking came the heightened awareness that childhood aggression is not just a short-term nuisance to teachers and parents that children "grow out of." Highly aggressive children, both boys and girls, of all classes and ethnicities are potentially at risk for a range of negative lifetime consequences, including youth violence. Thus, an accumulation of research evidence, together with a rapidly escalating awareness of youth violence in this country during the 1980s, created a new urgency among practitioners, policymakers, and researchers alike to find the means to reduce excessive displays of childhood aggression.

One early unanswered question was how our growing understanding of attributions and memory stores might help children like Don and Cory reduce their aggressive behavior. In 1989, I set out to answer that question. The result was the BrainPower Program, one of the earliest intervention programs that capitalize on existing knowledge from theory and research on children's thinking. I subsequently implemented, evaluated, and elaborated my intervention program to serve children who are at risk for the development of

lifetime patterns of aggression and violence and the negative consequences that are all too likely to follow. In this chapter I will describe
the development of the curriculum, and in the next chapter I will
examine BrainPower's impact on children's thinking and behavior.

How Thinking Patterns Produce Reactive Aggression

The first step in the development of the BrainPower Program was to
accurately describe the processes that were targeted for intervention.
My colleague Sandra Graham and I worked out a simple model to
describe the possible pathways from negative outcome to retaliatory
aggression. I have used that model through the years to guide my
development of the intervention program. It is shown in its most
recent, elaborated version in Figure 3.1.

We initially imagined that when a child interacted with a peer
and that interaction created a negative outcome, the aggressive child
would begin a specific pattern of thinking. The negative outcome
would lead the child to immediately generate attributions of hostile
intent; these thoughts would generate feelings of anger and lead to
retaliatory aggression. The unique feature of this pattern of thinking
was the bias in favor of presuming hostility in peers. Therefore,
correcting the biased sequence from thoughts to feelings to behavior
at its earliest stage (i.e., attributions of hostile intentions in others)
would effectively reduce aggression. I expected the intervention program of attribution retraining to reduce or eliminate biased judgments of a peer's intent. Once the biased judgment was eliminated, I
expected participants who faced negative outcome situations with
peers to more frequently begin the attribution process with benign
(e.g., accidental) rather than hostile causes. In turn, aggressive behavior would decline, because, as research has shown consistently,
when negative outcomes are attributed to nonhostile causes, anger
and aggressive behavior are unlikely to follow (Orobio de Castro et

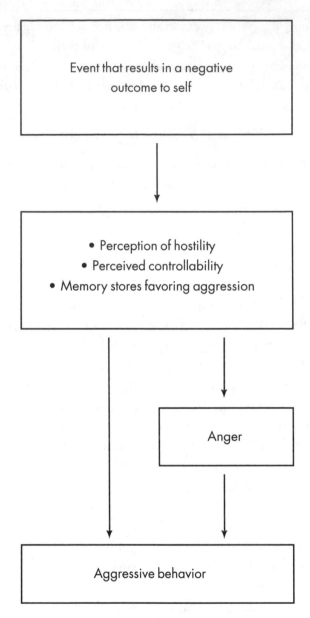

Figure 3.1. Two possible pathways to retaliatory aggression

al., 2002). This line of reasoning led me to conclude that attribution retraining provided a logical starting point in the development of an intervention package to reduce peer-directed aggression in elementary school.

However, I was not entirely sure about the role that anger might play in this sequence. The model in Figure 3.1 captures this uncertainty by including two possible paths to aggression. One path goes from thoughts through anger and on to aggression. The second, more direct path from thoughts to action does not require the experience of anger to create aggressive retaliation. The question for intervention was how much attention to devote to anger in the curriculum.

To clarify the question of anger, a research team tested the original model in a sample of middle school students (Graham, Hudley & Williams, 1992). We asked students to imagine themselves in a series of hypothetical situations that resulted in some kind of harm done to them by a peer. Typical stories included having their homework papers damaged, being ignored by a friend, and getting food spilled on their clothes. Some stories presented enough information to establish the intent of the peer who caused the problem. Other stories were intentionally ambiguous. We asked students to tell us how sure they were that the events happened on purpose, how angry they might feel, and what the best response was. We compared the responses from aggressive and nonaggressive students, both boys and girls. As we expected, aggressive children as a group reported a stronger preference for aggressive action, no matter the content of the stories or their reported level of anger.

In evaluating students' responses, however, we discovered that the influence of anger was not so clear after all. Although nonaggressive students' responses followed the pattern we expected, aggressive children's responses showed two distinct patterns. For stories with clear information about the peer's intent, both aggressive and nonaggressive children's responses followed the expected sequence from thinking about the situation and making attributions, to having feelings of anger, to expressing a preference for aggressive action. However, aggressive children's responses to ambiguous situations showed a novel pattern in which events led to anger, anger led to thoughts about hostile intentions, and these thoughts led to a preference for aggressive action. Thus, for aggressive children, anger was either a trigger for thought or the result of thought. Finally, and very important for my thinking about intervention, aggressive children's feelings of anger were not consistently related to their beliefs about peers' hostile intentions or to levels of aggressive retaliation. That is to say, aggressive children reported similar levels of anger when the negative outcome was identified as an accident and when it was identified as deliberate.

These results, like most research in social science, are open to several interpretations. I opted for the simplest, most direct interpretation to guide my design for the BrainPower Program. Thoughts about intentions and peers were consistently related to preferences for aggressive behavior, and these thoughts were systematically related to the content of the stories that we provided. Anger was a more unstable, albeit important element in the chain of events leading to aggressive children's behavioral preferences. I concluded that thoughts and attributions were a more stable regulator of children's behavior but accepted anger was a volatile but significant influence on both thinking and behavior. Believing that the results of this study reliably connected patterns of thinking to aggressive retaliation, I allocated a greater share of the intervention curriculum to helping children think carefully and accurately about their peers' behavior than to having children address their anger. However, I also included specific lessons on children's feelings of anger and how those feelings could interfere with careful thinking.

Aggression Reduction in Local and Social Contexts

Once I felt confident of the appropriate content of the intervention, I considered several approaches for delivering the program. When, where, and how could the intervention program best be delivered? I ultimately settled on a school-based intervention program and tailored the lessons accordingly. I reasoned that schools provided a structured schedule, an almost constant flow of program participants, and a broad range of support staff to implement the intervention (e.g., counselors, paraprofessionals, teachers). A school context would thus provide a rich, supportive setting for the intervention, and the intervention would also provide a useful service to the participating schools.

In the school setting, a program that enhances thinking skills in social interactions has the potential to help all children interpret and respond to the social world in a functional manner. More socially competent patterns of thinking provide students with alternative ways of perceiving interpersonal situations, defining acceptable responses, and enacting behavior. For children who already show especially high rates of aggression, the intervention may serve to prevent clinical dysfunction. If allowed to develop into a clinical conduct disorder, aggressive behavior requires intensive therapeutic services. This educational program is an early intervention model that is also a more cost-effective alternative to individual therapy. Overall, the net benefit for schools who implement this intervention program might be reduced levels of aggression and a more peaceful school climate, which should in turn enhance peer relations, adjustment to school, and overall developmental outcomes for children who are at risk owing to reactive aggressive behavior.

This single intervention strategy is not a panacea. Aggression is clearly the product of multiple social and personal influences that exist in the home, the community, and the individual child. The evidence clearly indicates that multiple interpersonal and intrapersonal processes (Huesmann, 1998), as well as community (Horn & Trickett, 1998) and family (Prinzie, Onghena & Hellinckx, 2006) environments, can contribute to the display of peer-directed aggression. An intervention like the BrainPower Program, which concentrates on individual children and their behavior, will be most successful as one piece of a comprehensive package of intervention strategies to reduce high levels of childhood aggression.

Overview of the BrainPower Program

I designed the BrainPower Program to change children's patterns of thinking about social interactions in order to reduce aggressive behavior directed at peers. The intervention curriculum comprises twelve lessons of about one hour each, with materials and activities appropriate for the upper elementary grades—that is, grades 3–6 (Hudley, 1994, 2001; Hudley et al., 1998; Hudley and Friday, 1996; Hudley & Graham, 1993). The central goal of the intervention is to retrain aggressive students to *start* from a presumption of accidental rather than hostile peer intent in negative social encounters. This goal is accomplished by altering the participants' perceptions of intent in negative social interactions with peers. See Table 3.1 for a listing of each lesson topic; the topics are discussed below.

My focus on intent in the intervention was guided by the theoretical relationship between perceptions of control and retaliatory aggression. I concluded from research evidence that aggressive children perceive negative social outcomes to be caused by events and actions that are controllable (and therefore intentional) by the peer(s) with whom they are interacting. Thus, the program focuses on training aggressive students to attribute negative outcomes to uncontrollable or accidental causes, particularly when a peer's intent is unclear or ambiguous.

Table 3.1. The BrainPower Program Curriculum

Lesson 1. Discusses goals and benefits of BrainPower Program.

Lesson 2. Presents intent attributions and how they shape behavior. ACTIVITY: Role-play peer interactions.

Lesson 3. Introduces the concept of nonverbal cues as an aid to intent detection. ACTIVITY: Play picture identification game.

Lesson 4. Discusses how one's own feelings may interfere with intent detection. ACTIVITY: Analyze story.

Lesson 5. Continues exploration of processes for intent detection with a focus on ambiguous situations. ACTIVITY: View prepared videotapes.

Lesson 6. Reviews the skills necessary for accurate intent detection. ACTIVITY: Create scenarios to demonstrate intent.

Lesson 7. Focuses on the idea that ambiguous situations do not really fit any one category. ACTIVITY: Review scenarios from Lesson 6 and story from Lesson 5.

Lesson 8. Discusses causation in social situations by contrasting controllable and uncontrollable causes of events. ACTIVITY: Analyze story endings.

Lesson 9. Addresses how to detect similarities/differences and categorize situations. ACTIVITY: Role-play peer interactions.

Lesson 10. Introduces appropriate action when responding to ambiguous situations. ACTIVITY: Brainstorm decision rules; role-play.

Lesson 11. Practices questioning skills. ACTIVITY: Role-play interviews.

Lesson 12. Reviews the concepts and skills presented in the program. ACTIVITY: Brainstorm strategies for remembering curriculum; receive certificates.

One of the unique strengths of this program is the nature of its development. I used what has long been referred to in the research literature as a constructive treatment strategy (Kazdin, 1980) and concentrated on attributional change as a starting point. That is to say, I isolated and identified the role of one pattern of thinking that has been reliably linked to aggressive behavior—specifically, a bias in attributions of intent. This theoretical and empirical basis allowed me to construct a curriculum, the BrainPower Program, with a clear understanding of both how and why it should successfully reduce children's aggression. I know with strong assurance from both psychological theory and empirical research with children that the "active" ingredient in this research-based program is the changes in children's thinking. However, let me reiterate that this program will be most effective as a part of a comprehensive intervention program that transcends a narrow focus on within-child factors and sees children's behavior from a broad ecological perspective.

There are three major components in the intervention. The first component (Lessons 2–5) strengthens aggressive students' ability to accurately detect the intentions of others. Through a variety of instructional activities participants learn to search for, interpret, and properly categorize the verbal, physical, and behavioral cues that are present in the behavior of others in social situations. Elementary school children as a group have not yet achieved mature levels of social interpretation and insight. Also, prior research makes it clear that aggressive children are particularly inattentive to the social cues that others display. Therefore, training and practice in reading and interpreting social cues can be beneficial to this age group, especially for aggressive students.

After the participants gain some skill in the classification and interpretation of social cues, they are ready for the second component of the intervention (Lessons 6–9), which is designed to increase the frequency with which aggressive students make initial attributions of benign intent in negative social encounters. The curriculum materials present both hypothetical stories and role-play situations that often but not exclusively illustrate ambiguous intentions from peers. Using these materials, students learn to use social cues to make their decisions about the intent of others. Remember that an attribution answers the "why" question (e.g., "Why did he step on my toe?"). Students in the intervention program learn to answer the attributional question with the information that is presented in the social encounter. Students are also taught to associate both the absence of social cues and an assortment of inconsistent cues in the same interaction with attributions to "uncontrollable" or "accidental" causes. This intervention does *not* teach children that all negative outcomes stem from benign causes; such a belief would be debilitating and dangerous. The goal is for participants to understand that an attribution to accidental causes is their first best option in the absence of clear and compelling evidence to the contrary.

The third component (Lessons 10–11) connects the meaning of intentionality to decisions about appropriate behavior in negative outcome situations. By this phase of the intervention students have gained some skill in assessing the social scene and a peer's intent. Now they apply their newly acquired skill in interpreting social information to understand their own behavior. Students learn to make decisions about the most appropriate behavioral responses to negative outcomes based on improvements in their interpretations of peers' intentions. They also learn to consider the social impact and consequences of their own behaviors. They are reminded that even when outcomes have a hostile intent, aggression carries with it a social cost (e.g., punishment by teachers and parents, reprisals by peers). Students are taught to generate decision rules about when to enact particular responses that seem to be appropriate to the presented social situation (e.g., "When I don't have the information to tell what he meant, I should act as if the situation were an accident"; "When another kid really tries to hurt me, I should find an adult"). If students can internalize more adaptive decision rules, they are more likely to maintain newly acquired processing skills over time and to generalize their skills beyond the intervention setting.

Lessons in the BrainPower Program

Lesson 1 is an introductory lesson to familiarize students with the content, format, and expectations of the program. The group leader provides students with a general introduction to the program's rationale, benefits, and activities. From the very first day, students are told that the group will talk about the ways we use our minds to control our behavior, and no reference are ever made to an individual student's history of behavioral difficulties. Rather, students are told they have been selected for a leadership program. Students also receive an orientation to group procedure and rules of conduct for the intervention sessions. They are told that they are expected to try their hardest, participate appropriately, and complete all activities. Finally, to establish a sense of community, the group leader and the students participate in an icebreaker activity.

In *Lesson 2*, students are introduced to the concept of intent in interpersonal situations. The leader first elicits spontaneous definitions of the word and then reinforces the meaning by reading a prepared dictionary definition. A series of brief examples (e.g., "If you set your milk carton on the ground and two kids chasing each other kick it over, can we say that they intended to spill your milk?") introduces the distinction between key intents: accidental, helpful, and hostile. Next, the group reads and discusses a story of a student who retaliates inappropriately after incorrectly assuming that a peer bumped him or her "on purpose"—that is, with hostile intent—in the lunch line. After the students read about the bumping, the retaliation, and the consequences for the aggressive student, the leader focuses the discussion on the ways in which inferences of intent might determine behavior. For the last activity, students role-play situations that might lead to misattribution of hostile intent and discuss causes and consequences. The initial homework assignment asks students to keep a log for the next four days of what they think are instances of errors in judgments of intent.

In *Lesson 3*, students learn ways to detect nonverbal cues and pair them with the major categories of intents (hostile, accidental, helpful). The leader begins by eliciting ideas about how to "guess" a person's intent without actually being told what it is (e.g., look at the face, listen to the tone of voice, watch for gestures). Then the students play a game with photographs in which they identify intent from facial expressions. They must select faces that illustrate the intent expressed in contrasting pairs of sentences (e.g., "I stepped on your toe because I was talking to another kid and didn't notice you sitting there" versus "I stepped on your toe to get you back for what you said about me"). This activity leads to a discussion of the types of facial cues that are useful in the accurate detection of another's intent. Students consider the look of facial features such as eyebrows (e.g., turned down for anger) and lips (e.g., open to show surprise) as aids to interpreting the intent of another.

After the picture game, students discuss the homework logs and act out some of the situations that they logged. The group leader guides the discussion to help students incorporate ideas about behavioral and facial cues as guides to understanding intent. For homework, students complete an "intention detective code book." They have to think about three people they know reasonably well (friends, family members, teachers) and describe each person's familiar social signals (e.g., "How do you tell when they are angry, surprised, happy? How do you know when they are being helpful; when they have made a mistake; when they are rushing?").

Lesson 4 addresses the importance of knowing one's own feelings. The leader opens a discussion about how we all feel when something bad happens to us. The conversation is guided by the idea that negative outcomes often generate bad feelings, and these feelings can interfere with the accuracy of intention detection and lead to misattributions. Students first read a short scenario with a negative outcome ("Another student pulls out your chair to clean under the desk when both of you are not paying attention to each other, and you sit down hard on the floor") and discuss how they would feel in that situation. The discussion focuses on the difference between having feelings about a situation and attending to the cues present in a situation (the scenario is written to suggest that moving the chair at that precise moment was most likely an accident). The students break into two groups and read a longer, more complex story about two friends who have a series of misunderstandings based on misattributions and anger. Each group has to report back how they think the events in the story are influenced by attributions and by anger. Students are encouraged to compare misunderstandings in this longer story to the data from their homework, which suggest that they *can* avoid misunderstandings by reading the social cues that are familiar to them. For homework, students receive a sentence completion task that helps them identify the influences of anger on misattributions. After reading a series of brief scenarios, students complete unfinished sentences to identify feelings that would likely be elicited ("When that happened I felt＿＿＿＿＿") and information that they can gathered from the text ("When that happened I knew ＿＿＿＿ because ＿＿＿＿").

By *Lesson 5*, students bring together their understanding of intent categories and social cues and learn the significance of an ambiguous situation. The group leader conducts a brief initial discussion to review the three categories of intent and the categories of social cues that have been discussed for the last two lessons. Next the students read a complex scenario that presents several conflicting cues and portrays a variety of behaviors and errors of judging intent. In the subsequent discussion, students talk about the causes and consequences of the behaviors of each of the people in the story and how angry each of the story participants might feel. During this discussion the leader introduces the concept of ambiguity. Then the students view a set of four short videos using child performers that illustrate the four types of intentions in peers: hostile, accidental, helpful, and ambiguous. (These videos were prepared with volunteer help from a high school media literacy class, for which I am eternally grateful.) The concept of ambiguous intent is explored and contrasted with the other three types of intent. For homework, each student has to prepare to discuss two situations in which the intent of another person was misjudged and describe how attention to some of the social cues discussed might have helped avoid misunderstanding.

In *Lesson 6*, students first discuss their own ideas about the four types of intentions as they present their homework. Then, after reviewing the four prepared videos from last week, they create four original scenarios that the leader transcribes (or video-records, if equipment is available). The goal is for students to demonstrate their understanding of the differences between helpful, accidental, hostile, and ambiguous peer intent in social interactions.

Students begin *Lesson 7* by reviewing their four scenarios show-ing intent. The leader asks students to look carefully at each scene to find the cues that tell them which intent is being portrayed. Discus-sion of the ambiguous scene focuses on the idea that ambiguous situations do not fit into any one of the three familiar (hostile, accidental, helpful) categories. Students discuss the usefulness of equating ambiguous with accidental intent. Using the story with ambiguous intent introduced in Lesson 5, students weigh the costs and consequences of making an initial attribution to any of the defined categories (accidental, which allows one to gather more information; hostile, which might require responding with aggres-sion and then dealing with consequences from adults and peers; helpful, which may require more information and might create some confusion in peers). For homework, students receive an un-finished story to complete. In the story, which has an ambiguously intended negative outcome, two boys are playing with a game that is about to be confiscated by a teacher. One of them hides the game, but the other one, the owner, is later unable to find his friend and retrieve his property. Students are expected to write two endings for the story, one presuming a hostile and the other an accidental intent.

Lesson 8 begins with each student presenting the two endings created for the Lesson 7 homework. Students discuss the situation in which the peer apparently disappears with the game and the likely feelings of the owner of the game. They assess the available social cues, which are deliberately restricted in the text of the story. Students next evaluate their own responses. Subsequently, two prepared endings are read and discussed: one with circumstances beyond the friend's control ("My mother came for me and took me to a doctor's appointment before I could give it back") and one with an action under the friend's control ("I wanted to play with it some more"). The discussion focuses on helping students compare and contrast critical features of controllable and uncontrollable causes and the kinds of social cues that might be most helpful in deciding when a cause is under someone's personal control or not. Students next review three stories introduced in previous lessons (including the very complex story from Lesson 5) to locate the cues that reveal whether a cause is controllable and how participants' feelings might influence their actions. For homework, students receive a short but complex scenario to analyze.

In *Lesson 9,* after discussion of the homework analyses, pairs of students role-play six prepared situations (e.g., a peer spills milk on you in the lunchroom). After each scene, the students discuss the cues and, using the cues, classify the scene by intent. Discussion focuses on grouping ambiguous scenes in the accidental category, using a cost-benefit analysis. For homework students are asked to record several situations in which a peer's intent is hard to judge, including the action the peer took in response to the situation.

For *Lesson 10,* students present their findings from their own experiences. In the presentation, they analyze and explain the category of intent for each of their situations (every student has to present at least one situation). The leader then introduces the idea of how students can use this information in everyday life as a guide for planning actions. The discussion makes the point that using intent analyses can lead to behavior that is appropriate to the situation and that does not bring about negative consequences from adults and peers. Then students brainstorm decision rules for each possible intent (e.g., If an action is accidental or ambiguous, choose a verbal response that seems to fit: ask a question, describe the situation, ask for help from an adult). Finally, students role-play ambiguous situations and try three different behavioral responses. In discussion, they decide which alternative might be the best choice. The leader makes clear the cause-effect relationship between social behavior and personal consequences. For homework, students, as for an earlier lesson, record two situations in which someone's intent is misjudged, but this time they decide whether the behavior was appropriate for the situation.

In *Lesson 11,* students discuss their homework analyses. The leader then discusses a new skill—asking questions—by asking why questions work well sometimes but not others (factors: how you ask, what your tone of voice is, what your other nonverbal cues might be, what you ask, how angry each person is, who else is listening). Pairs of students then role-play two ambiguous situations. One student role-plays the peer instigator, and the other an interviewer, who tries to determine probable cause and intent by asking the peer instigator questions. The students work through the role-plays to imagine how they might really feel if someone were asking them questions or if they were really asking the questions. They also consider how they would behave based on their judgments of the peer instigator's intent, which they are to determine based on the questioning process. The goal is to link the abstract rules for analyzing situations and deciding behavior to concrete life experiences. For homework, students are to practice asking questions in their regular interactions.

Lesson 12 is a general summary and review of the program concepts and skills. The curriculum provides a set of review questions (e.g., What is intent? What are the four kinds we have discussed? What are the ways we can detect the intent of others? Why is it sometimes hard to detect the intent of others? What is ambiguous intent? Why is ambiguous intent different from the other three? What are some appropriate actions in an ambiguous situation?). Then students brainstorm strategies to help them remember to use the points discussed once the program is over. Some suggested questions to ask oneself are "What would I do if this were an accident?" "Are my feelings getting in the way of good judgment?" As a last activity, students receive certificates of participation in a ritual of some kind that can be devised by the local leader.

In sum, the BrainPower Program curriculum provides: (1) specific activities for understanding the concepts of intent and ambiguity in interpersonal interactions; (2) practice in identifying intentionality in others from a range of verbal and nonverbal social cues; (3) specific activities for distinguishing between intentional and unintentional outcomes; and (4) practice in making attributions and generating decision rules about how to respond given attributional uncertainty. The program focuses entirely on peer-directed social behavior and uses familiar playground situations typical of elementary school social life. The presentation is designed to be entirely task focused, with no reference to an individual student's history of behavioral difficulties. The curriculum emphasizes the personal and social benefits of nonaggressive responses in order to enhance students' motivation to spontaneously use trained skills (Bierman, 2004).

Implementation of the BrainPower Program

The BrainPower Program has been conducted as a school-based program of small-group instruction (Hudley, 1994; Hudley et al., 1998; Hudley & Friday, 1996; Hudley & Graham, 1993), as well as an after-school program (Hudley, 2001). Sessions can be convened in any quiet place separated from the regular activities in the classroom or recreation area. The site should have tables and chairs as well as a blackboard, an overhead projector, or some other means of recording and displaying information for the entire group. Groups of six to eight students should meet twice weekly in sixty-minute sessions for a total of twelve sessions. Each group should consist of no more than five excessively aggressive and no fewer than two nonaggressive students. The nonaggressive students participate in the program in order to enhance the benefits for both themselves and their more aggressive peers. The presence of nonaggressive students serves to (1) eliminate the possibility that the aggressive participants will be stigmatized as "bad" students, (2) give aggressive participants the opportunity to interact with positive peer models, and (3) give nonaggressive students the opportunity to change their attitudes and behaviors toward the aggressive students as they progress through the program together. This kind of interaction between aggressive students and their peers is considered necessary if program gains are to persist outside the intervention setting. The opportunities for interaction are also useful in counteracting the self-perpetuating negative effects of a reputation for aggressive behavior on aggressive children's interactions with their peers (Bierman, 2004; see also Chapter 4).

The most rigorously conceptualized and carefully developed intervention is still no better than the measurable outcomes it can produce. This leads us to the most important question concerning the BrainPower Program. How successful has it been with students? What exactly has the program been able to do for aggressive children? Over the past eighteen years I have examined the impact of this intervention with a variety of intervention group leaders and in a variety of settings. These are discussed in the next chapter.

CHAPTER 4

Research on the BrainPower Program
How Effective Is It?

The ultimate test of any program intended to improve children's lives is how well the program produces positive outcomes or prevents negative outcomes. While a clear theoretical model and a strong research base may be an important foundation for high-quality intervention programs, "the proof is in the pudding," as the saying goes. So it is probably no surprise that after developing the BrainPower curriculum, I spent the next eight years examining the ability of the program to improve children's behavior. I have examined the program in both a school-based and an after-school context. This chapter presents the results of three studies that have established the ability of the BrainPower Program to reduce current levels of aggression and inhibit the development of future aggression.

Attributions and Behavior Change

Once the BrainPower Program curriculum was developed, my first research task was to evaluate the theoretical foundation by answering two interrelated questions. Guided by the theoretical model set out in Chapter 2, I wondered whether the curriculum could change children's attributions and, further, whether changes in attributions would relate to reductions in aggressive behavior. To effectively prove that an attributional bias is one of an admittedly complex set of influences on aggression, I had to demonstrate that the behavior (i.e., aggression) could indeed be influenced by the thought process (i.e., attribution). That is to say, if the curriculum could change children's attributions in a positive direction and if these changes were followed by reductions in aggressive behavior that were not evident in appropriate comparison groups, I could conclude that the earlier change in thinking probably caused the later behavioral change. An affirmative answer to both of my research questions would demonstrate that the model accurately represented a causal relationship between thoughts and actions.

When I began to construct, implement, and evaluate the Brain-Power Program, researchers had not yet attempted to change attributions in aggressive children. However, a good deal of research had already been done demonstrating that attributional change programs could improve students' engagement in academic tasks (Forsterling, 1985) and reduce clinical depression (Harvey & Galvin, 1984) well before I began developing a similar program of attributional change to reduce childhood aggression. Given these positive results in the academic and mental health domains, I saw the intervention curriculum as a wise approach to investigating changes in children's social behavior while at the same time addressing the very serious problem of childhood aggression in school.

First Steps

The first implementation (Hudley, 1994; Hudley & Graham, 1993) was in a highly controlled, experimental study designed to establish BrainPower's ability to change children's thinking. Participants included 108 boys who were enrolled in grades 4 through 6. These students received either the BrainPower intervention or an academic enrichment program that taught critical thinking skills primarily through science and social studies activities. A comparison group did not receive any special attention during the intervention period. The three groups contained roughly equal numbers of boys.

This particular three-group research design made it possible to separate the effects of participating in another special program from the unique effects of participating in the BrainPower Program. With just an intervention group and a comparison group, I would have had no way to tell whether behavior change was in response to the general opportunity to receive special attention or to the BrainPower curriculum. By adding a second "special" group, I could compare changes in aggressive behavior for all three groups of students: those in the BrainPower Program, those who received unrelated academic enrichment in another special program, and those who received no special attention. Based on my model, I expected that only the BrainPower participants would improve in their behavior as well as reduce their attributional bias.

Because my research grows out of my interest in and concern with the healthy development of ethnic minority youths, I selected inner-city, minority schools as my intervention sites. For this first study I also concentrated on boys. The evidence is overwhelming that beyond the preschool years, males are substantially more physically aggressive than girls, although this gender difference is decreasing. Physical aggression is seen as a major problem in schools, both in the classroom and on the playground, by students, parents, and teachers (Coleman, 2006), as well as by the public at large (Rose & Gallup, 2003). Therefore, boys seemed to be the appropriate population for the initial study.

I chose to concentrate on elementary school students based on research on the development of aggression throughout life. Late childhood and early adolescence seem to be a time in development when aggressive behavior becomes a relatively fixed pattern that persists throughout the life span (Loeber et al., 2005). I reasoned that working with children just prior to this critical period would most likely allow me to identify students who were at greatest risk for developing lifelong patterns of aggressive behavior just when they were becoming a serious problem in school. In addition, students of this age group have developed the cognitive capacity and the language skills to participate in the intervention activities more effectively than younger children are able to do.

Selecting the participants. I selected participants from two elementary schools in southern California serving a mix of working-class and economically distressed communities. Both schools also enrolled student bodies that were more than 80 percent African-American. Given these demographics, I decided to confine the sample to African-American students to make any results more clearly interpretable. To identify students who were clearly showing aggression among their peers, I collected ratings from both teachers and classmates in seventeen separate classrooms across grades 3–5 in the two schools during the latter part of the spring semester.

Teachers rated every student in their respective classrooms on eight behaviors that are typical of childhood aggression (e.g., "This child starts fights" and "This child overreacts to accidental hurts with anger and fighting"). For each item of the behavior measure (Coie & Dodge, 1988), teachers rated students on a five-point scale, with higher numbers meaning more aggressive behavior.

All students in the same seventeen classrooms completed a peer nomination questionnaire during a classroom session. Using a class roster, children wrote down the names of the three students in their class whom they liked most, the three whom they liked least, and the three who best fit each of five behavioral descriptions. Three of these behavioral statements described aggression (i.e., "starts fights," "gets angry quickly," "disrupts the group"), and two described positive behaviors (i.e., "works well with others," "is helpful to other students"). Children were encouraged to be honest in their responses, and they were assured that their answers would be held confidential.

To reduce the potential for later conflict among students due to negative evaluations, the classroom procedure was immediately followed by a competitive game with prizes, which served as an engaging distraction from the nomination activity.

Once these classroom procedures had been completed, I was able to combine the results and identify a well-defined group of boys. Aggressive participants were those who received lower than average positive behavior ratings and liking nominations from peers, higher than average disliking nominations from peers, and higher than average ratings of aggression from both teachers and peers. Thus, participants categorized as aggressive in this study were both perceived as aggressive at school and disliked by their peers. Nonaggressive participants had average or higher positive behavior ratings and liking nominations from peers, average or lower disliking nominations from peers, and average or lower ratings of aggression from both teachers and peers.

This was the research study that led me to Don and Cory, the two boys we met earlier. They were both participants in the BrainPower Program, as were two other participants I had the opportunity to talk to at the end of the intervention activities: Albert and Keith. All four of these boys initially were similarly perceived by teachers and peers as aggressive and were not very well liked. While Don received the greatest number of aggressive nominations in his school, Albert, who attended the same school, held that dubious distinction for his classroom. Cory received the greatest number of nominations of any student in fourth grade, while Keith was the third most nominated fourth grader at the school they both attended, a school with five classes of fourth graders. Yet, as we shall see, even among these four, opinions about how to manage social situations with peers were very different.

During the following fall semester, when the identified boys were in grades 4–6, seventy-two aggressive boys and thirty-six nonaggressive boys were randomly assigned to the BrainPower Program intervention, the academic enrichment group, or the no-treatment group. Participants in the BrainPower and academic enrichment groups were told that they had been selected especially to assist the school in evaluating a program that might be used with students in schools throughout the city. We conducted three intervention groups and three academic enrichment groups at each of the two schools for a total of six groups of each type.

Conducting the intervention groups. Each instructional group consisted of six boys, four aggressive and two nonaggressive. Nonaggressive students were included in the groups for two reasons, as I suggested in Chapter 3. I wanted to avoid stigmatizing the students who participated as "bad kids." Our aggressive participants already had a negative reputation with everyone, teachers and peers, alike. To single them out in this way would have been to cement and validate this reputation, leaving them and the program vulnerable to what are known as iatrogenic effects. Simply stated, intervention programs can sometimes cause the very effects that they are trying to reduce (McCord, 2003). A program that involved only aggressive students would run the risk of allowing children in the program to encourage and reinforce one another's negative behaviors and beliefs, a form of iatrogenic effect known as deviancy training or peer contagion (Dishion & Dodge, 2005). Aggression researchers have long documented the tendency for groups of aggressive boys to react more positively to discussions of antisocial behavior than do nonaggressive boys, while groups of nonaggressive boys react more positively to discussions of socially appropriate behavior (Dishion et al., 1996). I was diligent in working to avoid the possibility that participation in BrainPower would increase rather than reduce both aggressive and nonaggressive students' preference for and endorsement of aggressive beliefs and behavior.

I also included nonaggressive students to give aggressive boys the opportunity to interact with their more positive peers; such experiences benefit both aggressive and nonaggressive children (Bierman, 2004). Aggressive children gain benefits from programs that allow them to observe, interact with, and develop connections with positive peer models. Rather than providing the deviancy training that might occur in a group composed only of aggressive children, nonaggressive children bring an authentic peer voice to the conversation that expresses an alternative view that does not endorse aggressive behavior. Placing two nonaggressive students in each group also ensured that a positive worldview would be shared and supported by at least one other group member. At the same time, nonaggressive children in intervention groups would be able to reappraise their attitudes and behaviors directed toward aggressive students as those students gained positive social skills. As discussed in the last chapter, a reputation for aggression has a pervasive, self-perpetuating effect in aggressive children's interactions with peers (Rubin, Bukowski & Parker, 2006). Thus, nonaggressive participants become both positive models and potential allies in the peer world beyond the intervention setting.

I conducted the intervention groups with the help of graduate students in a teacher preparation program. Each group leader, after completing sixteen hours of training in the curriculum, led three BrainPower and three academic enrichment groups, distributed across both sites. Leaders took students from class during the course of the regular school day and brought them to an unused classroom on their respective campuses with tables, chairs, and a blackboard. Groups met twice weekly in sixty-minute sessions for twelve sessions. The intervention team and I met on a weekly basis for the duration of the intervention to discuss any questions and concerns around the implementation of the program.

Measuring program effectiveness. For this first intervention, I gathered information both before the start of the program and within one month after its conclusion. I measured participants' attributions about peer provocations, their teachers' ratings of their aggressive behavior, and the number of disciplinary referrals to school administrators that they received. For each of these measures, I expected aggressive boys participating in the BrainPower groups to show a reduced perception of hostile peer intent, less anger, and a lower incidence of aggressive behavior after the close of the intervention. After the intervention ended, I also had students participate in a frustrating laboratory task and conducted in-depth interviews with four aggressive students.

Changes in attributions were measured primarily using the same kinds of hypothetical scenarios that are typical in attribution research. Each student was individually presented with five stories that ended with a negative outcome for the main character at the hands of a peer. Each story presented a situation of destruction of property (e.g., a ruined homework paper), physical harm (e.g., a hard push by a peer while playing baseball), or social rejection (e.g., a planned meeting with a peer who never showed up). In each story, the peer's intent could be determined by using the cues embedded in the narrative. For example, in the homework story, the child had to imagine walking onto the schoolyard and setting his notebook down, only to have an important homework paper blow out onto the ground. A peer then steps on the paper, leaving a dirty footprint in the middle. The story concludes with one of four possible endings:

1. In the hostile version, the peer laughs and says, "You lose."
2. In the accidental version, the peer apologizes and says that he did not see the paper.
3. In the helpful version, the peer explains that he was trying to save the paper from flying into a puddle in the street.
4. In the ambiguous version, the peer looks at the paper and back to the child and says nothing.

Each student read and responded to five different stories (one each of accidental, hostile, and helpful intent and two of ambiguous intent) in a single session prior to the intervention program. At the close of intervention students received five new stories of the same type. For each one, four questions were asked about the hypothetical peer's intent (e.g., "Do you think he did this on purpose?") and two questions about felt anger (e.g., "Would you be angry with this person?"). These questions were rated on a seven-point scale. Participants also chose one of six behavioral responses ranging in aggression intensity from "Have it out right then and there" to "Do something nice for him."

This measure offers the most direct evidence of intervention success in changing students' attributions. Aggressive students who participated in the BrainPower Program became more positive in their judgments of the ambiguous stories by the end of the program. Sixty percent of the aggressive students in the BrainPower Program rated the ambiguous stories the same way the nonaggressive students did; none of these aggressive students increased their negative perceptions, and the overall group mean declined significantly. Ratings in the other three story types did not change significantly from pre-test to post-test.

Aggressive students in the academic enrichment and the no-intervention groups did not change their ratings significantly on any of the story types at the end of the intervention program. Only 6 percent of those in the comparison groups rated stories similar to the way all nonaggressive students did, 12 percent of the students in the other groups actually became more negative in their ratings, and the overall group mean did not change for each of the other groups. Group means for nonaggressive students across all of the groups showed no significant changes in any of the story ratings.

In summary, only those aggressive students in the BrainPower group reduced their story ratings to a level comparable to that of all nonaggressive students by the end of the program. Further, they were also the only aggressive students who showed no significant increases on any of these measures. The BrainPower intervention apparently not only reduces attributional bias but also counteracts a normative developmental increase in bias among some aggressive students.

To get a sense of behavior changes, I had each participating student's classroom teacher provide behavior ratings. Aggressive behavior was measured using the same eight questions completed by the previous year's teacher. Five new items measured positive behavior (e.g., "This child shares things in a group"), and four items measured academic performance (e.g., "This child has trouble completing work"). Each teacher completed rating scales the week before the start of the program and again the week following its conclusion. Although teachers were aware that some students were removed from class to participate in the study, they were not aware of students' intervention group assignments.

This measure of changes in student behavior offers evidence of program effectiveness that has the greatest practical significance. Teacher perceptions are especially important in the study of children's aggression, because teachers' judgments are arguably the most important standard for defining problem behavior in the schools. More than any other staff members in the school setting, teachers typically carry the institutionalized power and responsibility to pass judgment on their students. Therefore, the most effective intervention program will be one that improves student behavior as perceived by teachers.

Following the intervention, teacher ratings of aggression were significantly more positive in comparison to pre-intervention ratings only for aggressive boys in the BrainPower group. No such results were evident for teacher ratings of aggressive students in the comparison groups or any of the nonaggressive students (whose ratings remained uniformly positive). In addition to looking at changes in behavior for the groups as a whole, I was especially interested in how the intervention influenced individual students' behavior. Thus, in addition to statistical analyses, I also analyzed individual ratings using a technique developed to measure the success of clinical treatment (Jacobsen & Truax, 1991). The technique measures change that moves participants in clinical treatment away from a dysfunctional population and into a functional or normative population. For this study, I compared teacher behavior ratings that were gathered after the intervention for all students to the ratings of nonaggressive students collected prior to the intervention.

Although teachers continued to rate the majority of aggressive students more negatively than they did their nonaggressive peers, more than twice as many BrainPower participants (24 percent) as students in both comparison groups (9 percent) achieved ratings that were similar to those of nonaggressive students. Also, three times as many comparison students (12 percent) as BrainPower participants (4 percent) showed behavior that was worse than their behavior before the intervention began. Teacher ratings of behaviors other than aggression were not affected by the intervention for any group, and there were no changes in teacher ratings for nonaggressive students.

The research team also examined discipline records to assess how often participants were sent to an administrator's office for formal action. Administrative logs were reviewed for the school year immediately preceding the experimental intervention and for the school quarter immediately following the intervention (January–March). These records represent referrals for all types of discipline events, including physical and verbal aggression, disruptive classroom behavior, deliberate disobedience, theft, and vandalism.

The results were less clear for this measure, no doubt because school records included a very broad variety of misbehavior beyond acts of aggression. Prior to the intervention, aggressive participants were almost three times as likely to be referred to the office as nonaggressive participants. Aggressive students in the BrainPower group experienced the greatest absolute reductions in office referrals three months after intervention. Although aggressive boys overall continued to be referred to the office at significantly higher rates than the nonaggressive boys, 20 percent in the BrainPower group had rates of referrals that were similar to those of nonaggressive students. There were no reductions in referrals for aggressive students in the comparison groups. Referral rates for the nonaggressive students remained unchanged and were well below averages for aggressive students.

After the intervention, aggressive participants in all three groups completed a laboratory task that was actually an insoluble puzzle. Two students, one participant and a matched nonparticipant, had to work together. Both received simple grid maps showing various buildings and streets; they were told that they would take turns being direction giver and direction receiver. If the receiver arrived at a destination known only to the direction giver, he won a prize. On the first turn, the BrainPower participant always received directions and attempted to win the prize. Unbeknownst to either child, the two maps were slightly different, so incorrect directions were given, the destination was not reached, and no prize was awarded.

An observer unobtrusively recorded the BrainPower participant's verbal responses to the other student's instructions. Each response was later classified into one of four types: (1) neutral, defined as nonjudgmental statements to the peer or to the adult experimenter (e.g., "That road is a dead end"); (2) complaint, defined as negative comments regarding the subject's own performance (e.g., "I can't do this"); (3) criticize, defined as negative remarks to the peer about his performance (e.g., "You obviously don't know how to read a map"); and (4) insult, defined as negative personal comments directed toward the peer (e.g., "You're dumb").

At the end of the unsuccessful turn, the BrainPower participant was asked to rate his judgment of the direction giver's intent and to assess his own feelings of anger. Once these measures were collected, students took two additional turns. On both of these turns, the direction receiver successfully reached the destination, and both participants received comparable prizes.

For this insoluble puzzle task, aggressive boys who had participated in the BrainPower Program rated their partner's intent much less negatively than did aggressive boys in the two comparison groups. Similarly, boys in the BrainPower Program reported less anger toward the direction giver, although none of the children reported feeling very angry during this task. Among the verbal responses of BrainPower students, neutral comments dominated (61 percent of responses), and not one of these children resorted to insult. Among aggressive boys in the two comparison groups, the four classes of behavior were more evenly evoked, and one in six responses (16 percent) was classified as an insult.

For the four BrainPower participants interviewed individually, all within six weeks after the close of the intervention program, I randomly selected one student who received greater than expected teacher ratings of aggression and one student who received lower aggression ratings than expected from each of the two school sites. I asked all four of the students to tell me about how they got along with their peers and what they did together with their peers. Subsequently, I had each one describe a specific conflict or disagreement with a peer that had occurred recently. Don and Cory were the two participants whose behavior was unchanged by the intervention.

Don's perceptions of peers' intentions were quite negative and relied almost entirely on his own biased perceptions and little on actual evidence. He had a perception of his standing with peers that was in stark contrast to the ratings that he received from classmates. Don insisted that he rarely had any fights, arguments, or other difficulties with peers, commenting that most other students got along well with him. The only conflict he could think of during our conversation was the book-bag incident. This boy appeared to have significant disruptions in his peer relations and to make decisions based on deeply ingrained attributional biases. It is no surprise that a program as brief as BrainPower had little impact on his behavior.

Cory's behavior also remained highly aggressive. Post-intervention teacher ratings indicated that Cory actually increased in his tendency to threaten and argue with peers at school as the semester progressed. When describing the kinds of things he did with peers, Cory often spontaneously mentioned aggressive behavior. He described a group of friends he hung out with at school "so other kids won't feel like taking our stuff or starting anything with us." This group of boys may represent the beginnings of a deviant peer group composed of boys who were rejected by other students and came together to support one another in their antisocial behavior. Cory's worldview may also have been shaped in part by an older brother with whom he claimed to spend a lot of time and who apparently had been incarcerated for assault with a deadly weapon.

However, the two students whose behavior ratings were much better than expected provided a much more hopeful picture of BrainPower's influence. Albert, a fourth grader, showed concrete, positive evidence of change. When I asked him about a conflict with a peer, Albert described an incident that had occurred during the recess period right before our talk. One of his friends had pushed him down on the basketball court while they were playing on opposite teams. Almost immediately after Albert regained his feet the bell rang to end recess, and he and his friends left the court to line up with their respective classes. Although he felt the push might have been deliberate, Albert was not entirely sure, because "we were both running for the ball, and I got my hands on it. He pushed me in the back, and I just fell." He said that the incident might have been the result of "going for the ball to get in the last shot." However, it might just as easily have been the result of frustration at not being able to get the ball from Albert.

The problem of understanding the peer's behavior in this ambiguous situation seemed clear to Albert. Although he did not automatically assume it was an accident, neither did he assume that the peer had pushed him on purpose. He said that he was going to ask his friend at lunch time to explain the push. Based on that conversation, Albert would decide to either stop playing basketball with this person or just forget about the incident. Albert appeared open to an attribution of accidental intent for his friend's behavior but was still looking for more information on which to base his behavior. Most important, none of his plans seemed to include aggressive behavior.

My fourth interview was with Keith, a fourth grader whose ratings resembled those of a nonaggressive student at the end of the BrainPower Program. Violence and aggression seemed to be facts of his life. For example, he did not often play at the local park because "gangbangers are in there at certain times, smoking crack and acting wild. They take our balls and stuff if they catch us." Keith discussed disagreements with peers in the context of playing sports. Keith described being deliberately tripped while playing touch football in his backyard because his friend was losing so badly "that he stopped me any way he could. I know he felt really bad about getting beat. He didn't say sorry or anything either, but he wasn't trying to hurt me. He was just mad at losing." Keith told me that he simply shrugged it off because retaliation would only be appropriate if he had been hurt. Although Keith appeared to be incorporating intent information, it was not clear to me that he would have passed up aggressive retaliation if the outcome had been different.

To summarize, the two students who were rated by teachers as less aggressive after the intervention apparently took notice of presented social information in their interactions with other students. In contrast, students who remained highly aggressive were unlikely to cite available social information in explaining the need for aggressive retaliation. Instead, in justifying their aggressive behavior, both boys referred to their own general beliefs (i.e., attributional biases) that peers were behaving in a deliberately hostile manner toward them.

This first study clearly demonstrated that the BrainPower curriculum could indeed change aggressive children's attributions and that changes in thinking were followed by changes in aggressive behavior. Similar changes were not evident in either of the comparison groups or in the nonaggressive participants. I took this as evidence not only that the program was efficacious but also that our model accurately represented a causal relationship between thoughts and actions. However, this study was unable to establish how long behavior change might be maintained. All of the measures for this first study were collected within six weeks of the end of the program, and the teacher measures in particular were completed within the first two weeks after the intervention. So I turned to a study that was able to measure the effects of the BrainPower program over time.

Tracking Change over Time

The next study lasted over two years, so I was able to examine the duration of the effects of participation in the BrainPower Program. The study procedures (Hudley & Friday, 1996) were very similar to those described in the first study. I again confined participation to boys and included nonaggressive students in the sample. Participants were selected in a process that was identical to the one used in the first study. I also used the three-group research design, implemented the BrainPower and critical-thinking (academic enrichment) groups in a similar manner, and located the program in inner-city elementary schools.

However, this study was different in several respects (Hudley et al., 1998). This time students in grades 3–6 were included, and we drew our student participants from four rather than two schools. Most important, we followed the participating students for two years after the start of the intervention. Also, rather than relying on graduate students to lead the intervention groups, a team of two classroom aides at each of the four schools led the intervention and critical-thinking groups. Group leaders were all educational aides experienced in small group instruction who were nominated for the position by the principals of their respective schools. Prior to beginning the intervention, leaders completed forty-five hours of training over a three-week period. During training, leaders mastered the basic principles of attribution theory, became fully familiar with the content and methods of the intervention, and conducted simulated intervention lessons. Again, throughout the intervention I met weekly with the group leaders.

To examine the effectiveness of BrainPower, the previously described set of hypothetical stories again measured changes in attributions, and I again looked at school discipline referrals. Teachers also rated student behavior, but this time we used the Social Skills Rating System (Gresham & Elliot, 1990), which measures teacher's perceptions of students' self-control and cooperation as well as their aggressive behavior. Before the program began, immediately afterward, and for eighteen months after it was completed, we measured the attributions and the behaviors of 384 boys, 64 aggressive and 32 nonaggressive students at each of the four schools.

As with the first study, immediately following the intervention, aggressive students in the BrainPower Program reduced their ratings of hostility for the stories to much lower levels than they had been prior to intervention activities (Hudley et al., 1998). In contrast, ratings by aggressive students in both comparison groups either remained the same or increased in their perception of hostile intent. However, for the full follow-up period, BrainPower effects had diminished by twelve months to the point that the three groups did not rate the stories very differently at all. Over time, aggressive BrainPower students became more certain of hostile intent from peers, although their increases in perceptions of hostile intent were not quite as great as increases for aggressive students in the two comparison groups.

The teacher ratings of behavior showed a somewhat more successful pattern. Of all the student groups, aggressive students in the BrainPower Program showed the most improvements in teacher ratings of self- control at the close of the intervention activities, and these improvements were maintained over the follow-up period. Also, BrainPower students' ratings of hostility for the stories at the close of the intervention predicted teacher ratings of behavior at six months. The more positively the students rated the stories at the close of the BrainPower Program, the higher were their ratings of behavioral self-control from their teachers six months after the close of the intervention. Scores for the comparison groups of students remained fairly consistent, with a slight decline in teacher ratings of self-control for students in the critical-thinking group and a slight increase for students in the no-intervention group. Story scores for these two groups of students were unrelated to teacher ratings of behavior at any point. However, considering student scores as a group again masked the fact that some individual students' behavior had changed greatly because of the BrainPower Program, while other students seemed to have received little benefit at all. Therefore, as in the first study, I used a measure of individual change to look at the effects of the program over time.

As a group, the aggressive students never received teacher ratings that matched the levels for nonaggressive students. When looking at individual change, a different picture emerged. Two of five aggressive students in the BrainPower Program (43 percent) improved to levels close to that of nonaggressive students at the close of intervention, while only half as many in the comparison groups achieved similar results (21 percent and 18 percent for the critical-thinking and no-intervention groups respectively). By the end of the follow-up period, one in three BrainPower students had maintained their gains in teacher-perceived behavior, while the number of comparison students maintaining gains had declined by half (12 percent of students in the critical-thinking group and 9 percent in the no-intervention group). Finally, although in all groups some students' behavior declined to former levels by the end of the follow-up period, that decline represented 50 percent the students in the critical-thinking and no-intervention groups and only 28 percent in the BrainPower group.

These findings indicate that perceptions of hostility generally increased over time for students in elementary school, and teacher-perceived aggression remained relatively stable. Participation in the BrainPower Program seemed to improve on that natural developmental progression, but only over the short term. Since the intervention was relatively brief, it is not surprising that the duration of the effects was also short. It should not be a surprise that once any kind of services end, the benefits that came from those services are likely to diminish. Remember, too, that this brief intervention program targeted only one psychological process that plays a part in aggressive behavior.

These results can probably be most easily understood by considering the broader social context in which these students live their lives. Violent images and models are a fact of American life, history, and media, and a certain level of aggression is consistent with the values of the dominant culture at this point in time. For some of our program participants, violence and aggression may also be such a pervasive force in their social community that a relatively brief intervention at the individual level may not have much influence on their behavior once the program ends. I will return in a later chapter to this cautionary theme regarding the potential futility of psychological solutions to macrosocial problems.

However, the limitations of the BrainPower intervention, which was narrow rather than comprehensive in its scope and goals and disconnected to the students' broader social communities, also undoubtedly contributed to the limited duration of behavior changes. I was certain that this primary prevention program would have to be embedded in a more comprehensive intervention effort that includes family and community to successfully maintain change in behavior over time.

Moving Out into the Community

The move from school campuses was prompted by two primary goals. There is clear evidence that aggression is the result of multiple, complementary influences in the family, school, and community (Dodge, Coie & Lynam, 2006; Huesmann & Reynolds, 2001). Up to this point, my research program had shown that changing children's thinking could successfully reduce aggressive behavior in school. This evidence was clear support for the relationship between thinking and behavior that we had originally proposed in our theoretical model. However, my first goal was to make BrainPower a part of a comprehensive intervention addressing a broad array of the influences that shape children's behavior. I believed that such a strategy would enhance BrainPower's effectiveness over time.

I was fortunate to partner with the 4-H Youth Development program when I studied BrainPower as a part of a comprehensive, community-based intervention (Hudley, 1999, 2001, 2003). This partnership exemplifies my second goal. The 4-H Youth Development Program has been providing after-school enrichment programs to youths (ages seven to twelve) in the Los Angeles area since 1983, predominately in public housing projects. The overarching goal of the 4-H program is to develop children's intellectual, social, and behavioral competence and a sense of community among participants, both children and their primary caretakers. Families voluntarily choose to participate in the after-school program, although many are referred by school personnel and mental health agencies. Primary caretakers of participants are expected to contribute a minimum of three hours per week; many residents volunteer considerably more time.

The 4-H After School Activity Program (ASAP), serving from twenty to forty students per site, has activities five days a week, fifty weeks a year, between the hours of 2 and 6 p.m. The site programs are operated by a site supervisor, VISTA Volunteers, and volunteers from the housing project or community served by the program. For the duration of this study, site supervisors were typically young adults with some post-secondary education but not necessarily a bachelor's degree; VISTA volunteers were primarily college students. Community volunteers typically did not have a high school diploma.

Site staff plan and deliver a range of activities. All sites provide ninety minutes of homework assistance and thirty minutes of recreation activities per day, as well as site-specific projects related to personal social development, consumer education, creative arts, community development, and field trips to cultural and recreational venues outside the residents' own communities. These activities offer multiple opportunities for participants to experience academic and social success, as well as a sense of participation in, ownership of, and control over their own communities. For example, one 4-H site designed the playground that currently serves both the on-site preschool and the 4-H program. The municipal managing agency accepted the design. constructed the playground, and made sure that the student designers received appropriate awards and media attention for their accomplishments.

Families in the program seem to value the influence of 4-H on their children because children in public housing struggle with many challenges to their academic and social success, as well as to their very safety and survival. Social and economic isolation, high rates of violence, easy availability of drugs, early sexual experience, and minimal academic success are facts of life in public housing that pose a cumulative and highly toxic set of risk factors (Jarrett & Jefferson, 2004; McPhee, 2007). Families that live in public housing must be at the very bottom of the ladder of socioeconomic status, and in urban areas residents often are people of color. Their children also typically experience the cumulative effects of social injustice, community decay, and educational neglect that have been so frequently documented for poor ethnic-minority children living in urban areas. Poor children of color are also much more likely to experience violence and aggression in the schools, as both victims and perpetrators (Hudley, 1995), than their more privileged counterparts in affluent and suburban settings.

Middle childhood is typically the time when children establish the patterns of achievement and adjustment that will carry them through their school careers (Huston & Ripke, 2006). Living in hostile and dangerous environments in middle childhood can lead to social and emotional problems in adulthood, including violence and criminality, which will create enormous social costs and a needless waste of human resources. For those who provide intervention services, changing potentially dysfunctional developmental pathways becomes progressively more difficult and more resource intensive as children move into adolescence. Clearly, ethnic minority youth of elementary school age living in public housing provided me with a population for preventive intervention that was simultaneously among the most difficult to serve and the most in need of services. In short, this choice of intervention site was an especially exacting test of the effectiveness of the BrainPower Program, but it also provided a way to meet my goal of providing services to youth at highest risk for antisocial outcomes.

For this study, I incorporated the BrainPower Program into the ongoing activities at two sites in the 4-H After School Activity Program. Therefore, the study was very different in several ways from the preceding studies. Any student between the ages of eight and eleven, boy or girl, who regularly attended the 4-H program was able to participate in the BrainPower curriculum. The complex procedures for selecting participants that I described earlier played an important part in helping me establish the accuracy of the theoretical model that was the basis for the development of the intervention. But in the final analysis, organizations that serve children— places like schools, community programs, volunteer organizations, and recreational venues—must have programs that can be implemented fairly easily by people who do not have an advanced education. Further, programs must offer some reasonable expectation of success. So I wanted to implement BrainPower in a community program consistent with the way the intervention curriculum would be used once the research was concluded.

Before introducing the BrainPower curriculum at the two sites, the site coordinator and at least one volunteer at each site received four to five hours of training. Once they had completed training, the 4-H after-school staff (not including parents) conducted Brain-Power intervention groups of eight students; the typical 4-H activities also continued. As a result, BrainPower students simultaneously received aggression reduction activities as well as general youth development activities. However, intervention groups were conducted separately for boys and girls in order to better match the intervention curriculum materials to the participants' interests. Earlier research had already shown that physically aggressive boys and physically aggressive girls respond differently to peers' behavior

(Cairns et al., 1989; Whiting & Edwards, 1988), so the intervention activities were tailored to address the different experiences of boys and girls.

The BrainPower group consisted of fifty children (twenty-one boys and twenty-nine girls) attending the 4-H After School Activity Program at two public housing projects and the nearby public elementary schools. Forty students (twenty-two boys and eighteen girls) who lived in the same public housing and attended the two elementary schools but not the after-school program made up the no-intervention comparison group. The children ranged in age from eight to eleven years old, with an average age of nine.

To assess BrainPower's effectiveness, I again included the hypothetical stories to measure changes in attributions. Students also completed a fifteen-item survey to measure their beliefs about the use of physically aggressive behavior (e.g., "It's ok to hit someone if they insult you"). Also, both teachers and caretakers rated student behavior with the Social Skills Rating System (Gresham & Elliot, 1990). The primary caretaker of the family (usually the mother or grandmother) completed a survey of demographic characteristics (income, education, family size, etc.). I collected data at each site before implementation of the BrainPower Program and at six-month intervals for a year after the program was completed.

Over time, both boys and girls in the 4-H program reduced their belief that peers were acting with hostile intent in the stories (Hudley, 2001). For the comparison group, boys' perceptions of hostile intent became greater and remained higher than did the perceptions of 4-H boys and girls, but scores of girls in the comparison group declined to levels that were similar to those of 4-H boys and girls. Beliefs that physically aggressive behavior was an appropriate social strategy also changed over time, but in quite a different way. The beliefs of boys in the 4-H program became less supportive of aggression, while the beliefs of comparison boys stayed steady at levels higher than those of the 4H- boys. Although girls overall tended to be less supportive of aggressive behavior than any of the boys, girls in the 4-H group became slightly more supportive of physical aggression over time, while comparison girls became as supportive of aggression as comparison boys.

Again I had the opportunity to interview the students after the BrainPower Program was conducted. I was especially interested in understanding girls' opinions about physical aggression, for girls were particularly absent in the literature on physical aggression at that time. Girls' physical aggression has been much more frequently discussed in recent years (Putallaz & Bierman, 2004), although the research lags behind the larger literature on girls' relational and social aggression (Crick & Rose, 2000; Underwood, 2002).

Since my results suggested that girls overall tended to think more positively about physical aggression over time, I asked eight girls in 4-H to tell me what they thought was the right thing to do if someone acted aggressively toward them. Terrie, a girl in fourth grade, gave typical responses. When I asked what other kids usually did, she said they "fight, hit, and talk about people," and "girls do whatever boys do." In Terrie's mind, some kinds of physical as well as relational aggression were typical behavior for both genders. Interestingly, according to Terrie, boys "don't slap like girls do; that would be poof [weak, girly]." Interestingly, girls seem to have an even broader range of acceptable aggressive behavior than boys have. Slapping, which was apparently not all right for boys was, in her mind, completely appropriate for girls.

Terrie, along with every girl I spoke to, agreed that hitting was a main response used by other children in her school, by girls and boys alike, when they thought someone was being aggressive. When asked about her own responses, she first said she preferred verbal aggression as a strategy: "I would holler at them until they went away." Again, every girl I spoke to agreed that they would use some kind of verbal aggression (threats, shouting). Further, fully half of the girls to whom I spoke freely described physical aggression as something they would choose when they were confronted by a peer whom they perceived to be aggressive. Terrie was quite clear that she would "hit someone if she had to," meaning that if "hollering" did not stop a peer's behavior, she was comfortable with physical aggression. Overall, my interviews suggested that if girls have a propensity to see aggression where a peer's intent is benign, they will be as likely as boys to mount an unwarranted physically aggressive response, and that behavior seems to be supported by peer norms.

Parents of 4-H students rated their children as having more self-control, being more cooperative, being more responsible, and being less hyperactive then did parents of the comparison students. Teachers' ratings of self-control also improved over time for both boys and girls in 4-H. Teachers' ratings of comparison girls also improved, but comparison boys' scores declined consistently. After the BrainPower curriculum was completed, teachers' ratings of students' self-control were consistently related to students' thinking about hostile intent, but only for students who had participated in the BrainPower Program. The more these students had reduced their perceptions of hostility from peers, the more positively they were rated by teachers.

The most interesting result for school behavior, however, was related to student attendance. Following the intervention program, students in the 4-H program who had missed more than four days of school in a single semester generally received slightly higher ratings of physical aggression by teachers. Those who had more absences received average scores one point greater on a scale of 1–12 than did 4-H students who had missed fewer than four days. However, for comparison students who participated neither in the 4-H nor the BrainPower program, the average differences in teacher ratings were three points; students with poor attendance were seen by teachers as quite a bit more physically aggressive. Apparently, youth development and aggression reduction activities can provide some protection for children with problems; smaller problems can be prevented from becoming larger problems if children participate in appropriate, productive, and engaging activities.

Finally, parent and teacher ratings were not related. The differences in ratings of behavior between BrainPower participants and comparison students were greatest for teacher ratings of boys' behavior and parent ratings of girls' behavior. Teachers were more sensitive to the program's effect on boys' ability to behave in a school-appropriate manner, while parents seemed to be more aware of changes in their daughters' socially appropriate behavior in family and home settings.

Overall, a supervised program of activities after school seems to protect children in the face of high rates of crime that are a fact of life in public housing. This last study showed that changes in children's thinking and behavior can be achieved and maintained in a program that is already a normal part of their lives. I also established that the material can be tailored to be used by trained 4-H staff as a part of their regular activities rather than remaining a unique add-on program conducted by professional educators or university personnel. Thus, community-based programs that concentrate on positive development rather than targeting individual children's "pathology" appear to have strong potential for reducing or forestalling problem behaviors among children.

Lessons Learned

What lessons can we learn from the evidence presented in these three studies? Fundamentally, we now know that children's thinking can be changed with cost-effective educational strategies, and these changes in thinking can produce changes in children's aggressive behavior. This lesson is one of the most important and heartening messages that I have taken away from a decade of research. There is a chilling tendency in our society to give up on children much too quickly. The most disturbing turn of events in the past decade has been the policy to relegate children as young as thirteen to the adult criminal justice system (Stahl, Finnegan & Kang, 2003), although we know that children processed as adults are more likely to offend again than are children processed in juvenile court for similar crimes (Allard & Young, 2002). However, the ten-year-old child fighting on the playground does not have to become the adolescent delinquent or the assaultive adult; early behavior is not destiny. Concrete evidence that early behavior can be changed and more serious behavior forestalled is an important lesson indeed. Conversely, we must never forget the important corollary of this lesson. Left unaddressed, attributional bias and aggression in childhood will most likely lead to more, not less aggression.

The second very important lesson from the BrainPower evaluations is the knowledge that this program can be successfully embedded in a comprehensive youth development program that serves a broad range of children. As I have already discussed, the reduction of childhood aggression is much more than an individual psychological issue. Aggressive behavior is subject to many social and personal influences, and risk factors for aggression are present in many arenas of a child's life beyond the attributional process and peer relations that have been the focus of discussion so far. Living with neighborhood violence, for example, increases both aggression and attributional bias (Hudley & Novak, 2007), more so for girls than for boys (Farrell & Bruce, 1997) and more powerfully during middle childhood (Schwartz & Proctor, 2000) than at any other time in development. Similarly, parents who use harsh physical discipline or physically abuse their children teach by example that all relationships are threatening and dangerous. These children respond accordingly with aggressive behavior in peer relationships (Finzi et al.,

2001). Conversely, children who feel that they are valued by and positively connected to cultural and social groups (family, church, school) are far less likely to engage in antisocial behavior (Mannes, Roehlkepartain & Benson, 2005).

In sum, aggression reduction interventions that do not attend to the many environments (families, communities, peers, schools) in which children must grow and succeed will ultimately be of limited usefulness. The best programs will be those that positively and comprehensively engage the individual, family, school, peer group, and community. We now turn to a consideration of those broader contexts of children's lives and what comprehensive aggression reduction efforts might look like.

CHAPTER 5

Looking Beyond the Individual Child
What Schools Can Do

As effective as the BrainPower Program may be, the intervention is directed at only one of the many factors that shape children's aggression. An intervention that takes only the individual child as its focus is often not powerful enough to maintain changes in behavior over the long term and across several different settings, as we have seen. Without minimizing the importance of individual action, we must also recognize that the social situations in which the child lives, learns, plays, and encounters other people can make a powerful contribution to aggressive behavior. Influences as diverse as neighborhood crime and violence; harsh, physical parental discipline; and unsuccessful peer interactions may all play a part in the development and maintenance of children's aggressive behavior. Therefore, to be truly effective, programs of change must address a child's surroundings, or social ecology, as well as a child's behavior.

Our consideration of the social ecology of childhood begins in school. School is arguably the most important social setting in middle childhood, and school environments definitely make a difference in children's aggression. Reviews of school policies and practices show that schools with lax and inconsistent discipline policies, schools that do not address problems of bullying, and schools with generally high levels of incivility among students and adult staff are also likely to have relatively high levels of physical aggression among students (Osher, Dwyer & Jackson, 2004). Survey research also tells us that students' perceptions of such conditions influence their behavior. One such study with adolescents, for example, found that witnessing violence (e.g., fighting, bullying with weapons) in school was an important influence in students' decisions to engage in physically aggressive behavior, and this effect was stronger for girls than for boys (O'Keefe, 1997). Like the attitudes of our student Cory described in Chapter 1, such findings suggest that when physical aggression is the typical behavior in a school, students are often likely to believe that they should "do what they have to do" when confronted, and direct physical aggression is the response of choice.

However, schools that have vigorously pursued zero-tolerance discipline policies for physically aggressive behavior have also seen lower levels of motivation and interest in schoolwork among those students who do *not* run afoul of the policy; there are, for example, higher school-dropout rates among adolescents in schools with such policies. Perhaps more important, these negative effects are not accompanied by an overall decrease in physical fighting in these schools. It may be that some students see harsh punitive policies as successful displays of superior power and attempt to model these displays. Unfortunately, displays of power assertion are the exact opposite of the peaceful interactions that are the goal of such policies. Equally troubling, reviews of these policies show that ethnic minority boys (African-American and Latino) in multiethnic schools are punished with zero tolerance sanctions at rates far higher than their representation in either the population of students found guilty of fighting or the general school population. Finally, an unintended though unsurprising consequence is that zero tolerance at school may actually promote aggression and youth violence in the community by expelling those very children who are most in need of the benefits of a strong academic foundation, a caring school environment, and positive peer relations.

This evidence suggests that when schools are successful in crafting a climate of civility, one that reinforces the expectation that students and adults will maintain civil interactions, that climate helps to control students' aggressive behavior. The strategies for maintaining peaceful interactions must be positive; a punitive zero-tolerance policy may remove the most troubled and troubling students without improving the overall school climate. But if not the draconian measures of zero tolerance, then what? The overall goal for schools must be the two-sided process of reducing aggressive behavior and promoting a peaceful, positive climate. The two should not be viewed as separate goals; achieving widespread improvement in behavior at school is highly unlikely without a peaceful school climate. And because schools are complex social settings with complicated systems of student and adult social groups that are organized into networks of relations both between and among teachers and students that are sometimes but not always hierarchical in their arrangements, efforts to positively influence school climate and behavior must take into account all of the actors in the school setting.

When schools work to reduce aggression and promote a positive climate, they must focus on multiple kinds of strategies and programs. Many working in the area of behavior change in schools categorize prevention and intervention efforts according to a mental health model of classification described more than a decade ago (Institute of Medicine, 1994). The model is made up of a continuum of services, ranging from universal practices that benefit everyone in a given setting through specific long-term follow-up care for those with significant, diagnosable mental disorders. In this mental health model, the BrainPower Program would be defined as an "indicated preventive intervention" program, because it is designed to help those who show indications of potential future disorders. However, in a system as complex as a school, a variety of efforts will be needed to sustain a positive climate and reduce aggressive behavior. An intervention such as the BrainPower Program, which focuses on the individual behavior of a selected group of students, would be only one among such efforts. A number of specific strategies and complementary programs have been successful in helping schools reduce aggression and establishing and maintaining peaceful environments.

General Strategies for Schools

School strategies are specific direct actions that schools can implement or encourage for their students, teachers, and staff. Many strategies are simple, fairly obvious, and proven to work. For example, schools that promote and visibly honor student involvement in extracurricular activities tend to be places where both students and teachers are cooperatively involved in tasks that they find personally interesting and rewarding. Student involvement takes many forms at each level of school (elementary school, middle school, high school), ideally becoming more complex and self-directed as students mature. Activities may include various types of student government, hobby clubs (e.g., chess, garden, computer, photography), and creative organizations (e.g., drama productions, music groups, debate teams). Of course, such involvement also requires substantial commitment on the part of teachers, school administrators, and policymakers to make these involvement opportunities available for all students. A shared commitment to and enjoyment of activities that are mutually chosen and more flexible and egalitarian than traditional classroom activities seems to benefit both student-teacher and peer-peer relations (Fredricks & Eccles, 2006). Students at all points in their development benefit in many ways from involvement in extracurricular activities at school, evident in increases in positive behavior, decreases in negative behavior, improvements in peer relations, improvements in academic achievement and attitudes toward school, and the development of a positive self-concept.

Teachers who are involved in these extracurricular activities with students also benefit in several ways. Teachers gain important knowledge about their students' interests and ideas that can be translated into effective and engaging classroom instruction. Involvement with students in positive interest-driven activities also helps teachers sustain positive attitudes about schools and students, serving to protect against professional burnout. Finally, teachers are also able to pursue interests and avocations alongside their students.

One ubiquitous extracurricular activity, school athletics, seems more mixed in its ability to promote a positive school climate and reduce aggressive behavior. Schools with a broad range of available sports opportunities that can accommodate students at various levels of performance (elite to recreational) and encourage personal improvement and responsibility in their athletes seem to reap positive benefits in their overall climate. Schools that place developmentally inappropriate pressure to succeed on student athletes, turn a blind eye to or actively defend athletes' misbehavior, and provide school coaches who consistently model aggressive, power-assertive behavior seem to create a culture of intense competition, heightened aggression, and reduced civility.

Directly related to student involvement are school groups organized by students or schools specifically to promote nonviolence. Both the students and the schools often see an improved school climate and reduced levels of aggressive, antisocial behavior, including bullying, fighting, and teasing (Office of Elementary and Secondary Education, 2002). School groups will look very different in elementary compared to secondary schools because the most successful student experiences result when students take on developmentally appropriate responsibilities. Elementary school groups might create posters or Web sites, engage in classroom activities to promote peaceful interactions, and design peace pledges. Adolescents might organize assemblies, create informational Web pages, and work with the media or other community resources. The benefits of school groups promoting nonviolence seem to be embodied in the concept of empowerment. When students see that they are working in a true collaboration with teachers and schools to improve the social and emotional climate at school, they are more responsive, more positive in their behavior, and more likely to take ownership of efforts to improve their school than when their role is more passive or even resistant. Similar effects have been documented in research on collaboration in academic achievement.

A popular school program promoting student empowerment again comes with a caveat concerning potential benefits. Peer-led interventions, including peer counseling and peer mediation, are among the strategies that were widely embraced two decades ago when youth violence seemed to be spiraling completely out of control. Peer-led interventions are founded on two distinct assumptions. On the one hand, aggression in schools may be reduced if there are enough people in the social environment to listen to disputants and respond with strategies that support a peaceful resolution. According to this assumption, trained peers represent a significant human resource that can provide just such thoughtful listening and responding on a large scale in schools. A different rationale for peer-led programs assumes that the trained students provide a generally calming influence on the school climate rather than providing benefits through the actual mediation process. Those trained in peaceful conflict-resolution strategies are likely to use those strategies in resolving their own conflicts and therefore provide positive models for their peers. According to this line of thinking, increasing the number of peer mediators or counselors also increases the number of students who receive violence prevention education. The trained students disseminate their new knowledge to others by example in a process sometimes called the diffusion of the peace virus (Casella, 2000).

Over the years, scientific reviews and program evaluations have yielded mixed findings regarding the ability of peer facilitators to directly change the behavior of others and to improve school climate (Johnson & Johnson, 1996). While peer-led programs continue to proliferate in both elementary and secondary schools, the weight of evidence suggests that skill training is critical, that peers can sometimes exacerbate rather than help to resolve disputes, and that peer facilitators themselves benefit more from the programs than the disputants do. A report on youth violence from the surgeon general (U.S. Department of Health and Human Services, 2001) flatly declared that peer-led programs have consistently failed to show group-level effectiveness in reducing youth violence. On balance, peer strategies are at best analogous to programs of direct instruction for behavior change. Peer mediation and counseling are apparently able to improve school climate by virtue of the training that some students receive and subsequently use in guiding their own behavior, not by virtue of student mediators' direct influence on their peers.

More basic to the overall school context is the organization and management of school routines and activities. These can have a substantial impact on children's aggression. Unlike schools that suffer the debilitating effects of zero tolerance policies, schools with consistently and fairly enforced disciplinary policies that include clear rules, positive expectations, and reasonable consequences are able to provide an orderly yet nonoppressive climate for students and adults. These strategies have much more positive effects than an oppressive zero-tolerance stance when they provide a clearly defined, graduated hierarchy of sanctions that affirm the school's unwillingness to "throw away" students.

Discipline policies must be firm but also demonstrate that adults care about students; firmness and caring are the crucial ingredients that seem to best support a civil climate in schools. A civil school climate in which adults are skilled at maintaining a sense of basic order and safety has been shown to reduce student conduct problems when teachers also express appropriate care and concern about students' family and social difficulties. Conversely, in schools with a climate of conflict—where students do not respect teachers, and teachers are unable to maintain basic order and academic focus—conduct problems actually increase over time when teachers attempt to engage students in personal discussions (Kasen, Johnson & Cohen, 1990).

Beyond discipline, a school's clearly defined emphasis on academics seems to naturally inhibit student aggression. The school's unique mission is academics, and both students (Kitsantas, Ware & Martinez-Arias, 2004) and teachers (Binns & Markow, 1999) report that problems with student behavior pose a serious obstacle for educational activities in classrooms and in the school as a whole. As one might expect, organizing school environments in ways that maximize academic opportunities and achievement for all students minimizes student behavior problems (Kasen, Johnson & Cohen, 1990). Again, high expectations from adults are one key; all school staff, not only teachers, must communicate the clear expectation that they believe students can succeed. A challenging, developmentally appropriate academic curriculum is another important element of a positive school climate. Students must be engaged in appropriately challenging academic tasks if they are to develop their individual potential to the fullest extent possible.

I am often struck by substantial differences in student behavior in classrooms within a single school that can be traced directly to the quality of instruction and mutual respect evident in the classroom. Conversely, academic failure in elementary and secondary schools leads far too often to behavior problems, a lack of bonding to the school, and a devaluing of achievement striving (Graham, Taylor & Hudley, 1998; Morrison, Furlong & Morrison, 1997). One particular comment from a teacher in a severely underresourced school serving a public housing project sticks in my mind. "When we worry less about what kids cannot, should not, and must not do and concentrate on what they can and will do, they rise to the expectations. Kids never cease to amaze me; I am not sure I could overcome the problems they face and actually show up regularly, often early, for school."

Having small learning communities and career academies are two, often interrelated strategies that have been shown through a decade or more of research to improve behavior and academic achievement. Career academies are usually found in middle and high schools. Typically, core academic requirements (i.e., math, science, language arts) are paired with vocational courses for all students, and the whole curriculum emphasizes job-specific skills. Visits to, and later internships with, local employer partners tie classroom activities to the world of work and the prospect of a viable future for all students. Early career-exploration and counseling services help students plan effectively for post-secondary education and employment. The evidence suggests that individual career academies and small learning communities within larger secondary schools can establish a positive climate, improve student behavior and achievement, and reduce dropout. Student interviews across the country (Kemple & Snipes, 2000) provide details of a positive climate; students say that the atmosphere of trust, encouragement, and academic support from teachers and peers that is created within the small learning community increases their belief in themselves and their commitment to education.

In lower grades as well, small, personalized school arrangements seem to support academic achievement and a positive academic self-concept ("I am a good student"), which seem to work against aggression in school (Hudley, 1995, 1997a, 1997b), and the effects are strongest in schools that serve children who are most at risk for problem behaviors and school failure. I have spent time conducting research in three urban schools that were doing as poorly as so many of our schools seem to be in educating African-American boys. These schools drew my attention because of a novel program (which has since lost funding). African-American male students in grades 6 and 7 attending comprehensive middle-school campuses were placed in self-contained classrooms, each with to a maximum of twenty students. Students had specialized curricula for their four core subjects (math, social studies, language arts, science). For example, students read literature by African, African-American, and Afro-Caribbean authors as part of their language arts curriculum. Math instruction in problem solving included research projects calculating differential income, longevity, population distribution, and other factors as a function of gender and ethnicity, using data drawn from government publications at either their school or the public library. In my research I was able to demonstrate that, compared to African-American males in regular classes, students found these classrooms more supportive and encouraging of their educational aspirations; they were less likely to act out or skip school; and they believed that they were both intellectually and socially competent. I concluded that young men in these small classrooms with specialized, engaging material improved both their behavior and their achievement striving. The classroom itself provided a positive, encouraging climate. In interviews, teachers in this program described conscious efforts to develop such a climate to combat negative behavior. One of the teachers, for example, felt that by "keeping them busy and involved with things they want to know anyway, I minimize behavior problems." This teacher also included instruction in social interaction skills, "polite, respectful behavior which should be directed to others, whether they are teachers, friends, parents, strangers, whoever," as a regular part of the curriculum and accepted "responsibility as the classroom leader to model the behaviors toward students."

Finally, the importance of student social and emotional support services must not be overlooked. Counselors, social workers, school psychologists, school nurses, and parent volunteers all play a role in establishing a caring, supportive school climate. A caring school climate includes a sense of safety for all students. Recall that research with students in both urban and rural schools shows that children and adolescents who are victims of bullying, threats, and aggression from peers are very likely to behave aggressively themselves in future encounters with peers, and this dynamic relationship between victimization and overt aggression is sometimes stronger for girls than for boys. As discussed earlier, the reverse is also true; children who are aggressive are also likely to experience aggression from peers (see Chapter 1; Thomas & Smith, 2004).

To maintain the sense of order and security that works against aggressive behavior, adults should be visible and active as participants or monitors in school routines and activities (e.g., recess supervision, monitoring assemblies), and school staff should be aware of and monitor unsafe areas (Astor et al., 2005) of their campus (e.g., outdoor areas behind buildings). In addition to providing a sense of order and security, adults on a given campus can interact with students personally, greeting them by name and talking to them about their concerns. If they do this, students are likely to feel safe in the school, valued by the school, and bonded to the school. Adults should constantly informally and formally recognize and support students' efforts to improve or maintain positive school-appropriate behavior, and they should act affirmatively and visibly to deal with students' concerns about safety and security issues (e.g., bullying, threats). When we think about reducing children's aggressive behavior, we too often focus exclusively on changing individual children. The organization and climate of the school also make important contributions to students' behavior and should be carefully examined to identify appropriate interventions for encouraging and supporting positive student behavior.

The Classroom Environment

Classroom-specific strategies are just as important as whole school strategies for maintaining a civil, caring school climate. There is a consensus that maintaining a civil, calm classroom climate requires active planning, preparation, and caring. What is true for the school as a whole is true for the individual classroom; there, too, teachers must maintain firm, fair, and consistent discipline practices that students understand and support. Students should be given a developmentally appropriate role in constructing classroom rules of behavior. Very early in the academic year, teachers and students should spend class time building a sense of community with activities that include learning one another's personal preferences and interests, examining similarities and differences among classmates, establishing respectful rules of communication and sharing, and developing a classroom identity based on sharing and cooperation. Teachers and administrators must also take the lead in modeling caring, civil behavior toward students as well as toward other adults in the school. In the classroom program for African-American boys in the middle school that I described previously, for example, one of the teachers believed strongly that by allowing "the kids to participate in the decisions for their studies and for the rules of the classroom," he maintained student commitment to meeting both behavioral and academic expectations.

There is some evidence, although findings are mixed, that continued use of cooperative group-learning activities, if properly structured, can increase students' positive behaviors and reduce aggression and disruptiveness. Putting children in groups does not automatically benefit either learning or cooperative behavior. However, a long history of research on social behavior (Sherif, 2001) has concluded that conflict within and between groups can be reduced when activities require meaningful participation by all group members for successful completion. It may be that cooperative academic learning groups in classrooms are similarly able to reduce aggressive and disruptive behavior and build group solidarity when they are structured in a way that requires meaningful and sustained collaboration as well as academic skill development. Appropriately structured cooperative learning groups can provide a variety of social skills, including communication skills, perspective taking, negotiation, and compromise, which support positive engagement in both academic and social tasks (Gillies & Ashman, 2003).

There is much clearer agreement that the way classroom time is used can either forestall or increase aggression and disruptiveness. Teacher preparation programs devote explicit attention to the importance of managing transitions, the movement from one instructional activity to another. The goal is to minimize downtime, those periods during the day when students have nothing to engage them and may become bored and disruptive. Transitions that keep up the forward momentum of the instructional day seem to maintain student engagement in the classroom community and reduce disruptiveness and incivility. Similarly, lessons and assignments that engage students minimize the likelihood of boredom and detachment, which can fuel aggressive behavior. Long stretches of time with the teacher talking at students or students working independently on rote tasks are likely to lead to student apathy as well as behavior problems in the classroom and in the school more generally.

Comprehensive Programs

Aggression reduction programs that focus on the school environment rather than exclusively on individual student behavior have demonstrated evidence of effectiveness in improving school climate and reducing student aggression. In fact, coordinated programs that concentrate on both individual students with behavior problems (e.g., the BrainPower Program) and the broad school context typically yield the strongest benefits for schools and students. What follows is a brief review of two representative programs that attempt to change the broader school climate by engaging everyone in the building. These programs have been proven to be successful in supporting positive behavior, although each has a different program focus.

Peacemakers: a student-focused program. The Peacemakers Program (Johnson & Johnson, 1995, 2004) has been cited as a model program by the Substance Abuse and Mental Health Services Administration (SAMHSA) of the National Institutes of Health. This program, which incorporates many strategies common to conflict resolution programs, has been able to overcome the limitations of narrow focus and poor management discussed earlier in this chapter. The Peacemakers Program teaches conflict resolution skills to everyone in the school—students, faculty, and staff members. The program assumes that conflicts cannot be suppressed and will have positive or negative consequences depending on how they are managed. Therefore, everyone in the building must know how to negotiate to solve problems and reach agreements accepted by all disputants. All members of the school community use the same procedures for resolving conflicts, and teachers and administrators model constructive conflict resolution among themselves. Classroom teachers deliver the program content to students using case studies, role-playing activities, and simulated conflicts contained in twenty 30-minute lessons. Four lessons focus on the nature of conflict and its potential constructive outcomes; eight lessons teach students how to engage in problem-solving negotiations; and eight lessons focus on how to mediate schoolmates' conflicts. All adult staff receive the same material in written handbooks. Students and adults see that there is value in negotiation and compromise rather than a personal win, which can damage a relationship. In program activities, students also learn to do research and prepare to argue for their positions, a strategy that also promotes high-level reasoning. Teachers also learn to integrate program content into academic lessons in literature, social studies, and science classes. Each year, as students proceed to the next grade, the program is taught again at an appropriately more complex and sophisticated level.

The program's success appears to be the universal nature of the training. As discussed earlier, peer conflict mediation programs primarily benefit the trained children, not the peers with whom they work. The Peacemakers Program, by training every student, can deliver benefits uniformly across the student body at a given school. The results of a decade of research (Johnson & Johnson, 2004) indicate that students learn and retain program content throughout the school year, apply the conflict resolution and mediation procedures to their own conflicts, and use the procedures similarly in family and school settings. The more years that students spend learning and practicing the program content, the more likely they will be to use the procedures skillfully, both in the classroom and beyond. Thus, there is neither dependence on nor need for a small number of trained students to solve conflicts for others.

Effective Behavioral Support: a program for environmental change. Effective Behavioral Support (EBS) is a schoolwide model of discipline, organization, and management that is designed to minimize features of a school environment that support aggressive and antisocial behavior while increasing environmental supports for positive behavior. This model is grounded in an understanding that behavior is not solely a function of an individual but rather is produced by the interaction between an individual and a given environment (sometimes referred to as person-environment fit; Walsh, Craik & Price, 2000). To create this model an initial model of Positive Behavior Support (PBS), developed for children with significant disabilities who were extremely aggressive or who injured themselves in school (Meyer & Evans, 1989), was expanded into a schoolwide, comprehensive model that creates and sustains environments that promote and reward positive behavior. The EBS model is defined by several core elements (Sprague et al., 2001; Sugai & Horner, 1999) rather than a specified set of activities or curriculum materials.

Fundamental to the EBS model is its transparency. Both problem and positive behaviors for students and staff in a given school are clearly defined for everyone and may be directly taught to students. Everyone in the school community shares an understanding of what positive behavior should be and how positive behaviors contrast with problem behaviors. Too much of school discipline focuses on what students should or must not do; EBS makes it a priority to define and establish the opposite end of the behavioral continuum. Definitions of positive and problem behaviors are locally developed, which makes them both culturally and situationally appropriate for the environment in which students and staff interact and learn from one another. Thus, EBS is notable for its emphasis on policies and procedures that are culturally and socially relevant for a given context.

EBS requires a systemic analysis of environmental characteristics in a school that seem to produce unwanted problem behaviors (e.g., aggressive and antisocial behavior). The goal is to alter these conditions so that the problem behaviors are less likely to occur. For example, if a school can identify particular activities in which students tend to engage in physical or verbal aggression and conflict, an EBS intervention could be made. The teachers and staff would examine how to change the activities or substitute other activities that support positive behavior. Highly aggressive recess games (e.g., dodge ball) or intensely competitive activities with no adult supervision (e.g., basketball games during physical education class) might be either structurally altered or eliminated from the recess repertoire.

As well as examining antecedent conditions, in an EBS intervention the school is also asked to examine the environmental rewards or consequences that maintain problem behaviors and work to design environmental contingencies that encourage more positive behavior. These contingencies might include adjusting adult behaviors. For example, adults responding to student aggressive or challenging behavior might actually encourage such behavior by the positive attention that students receive. After an EBS intervention, institutional responses to such negative behavior might be revised—for example, students might be removed to private settings for discipline, which would restrict access to positive attention from peers. Also, the school might institute a routine for giving developmentally appropriate attention to positive behavior (e.g., teacher certificates of commendation in first grade or opportunities for leadership roles in high school).

New contingencies might also include changes to instructional routines. It may be that aggressive students are most disruptive on test days in a given middle school. The school might stagger exams across various days, rather than having all classes test students on Fridays (a very stressful practice for teachers and students). Or perhaps, as discussed earlier, teachers' efforts at cooperative learning are creating conflict among students, and some students are being actively rejected by peers in academic tasks and in the broader social environment of the school. In an EBS intervention, teachers and administrators might be asked to reflect on their policies and practices to determine more effective ways to structure group activities and perhaps seek appropriate in-service training to improve instructional skills in this area.

Staff are generally expected to participate in training and to regularly share feedback about effective implementation of the EBS intervention at their school site. The model is a collaborative, locally defined, schoolwide effort, and a given school site must commit to coaching and technical assistance for effectively implementing the intervention, monitoring and evaluating ongoing intervention activities, and receiving periodic review and retraining as necessary to maintain any gains that are achieved. This also implies a commitment to staying with the intervention over the long term and developing internal systems of evaluation for monitoring and assessing the intervention's effectiveness.

The nature of the EBS program assures that evaluation data are collected consistently, and evaluation data on schoolwide EBS initiatives are thus far positive. Although this research is relatively new, early published studies of some of the first programs to be implemented have provided promising results (Safran & Oswald, 2003). Programs evaluated using a combination of teacher ratings, archival data (e.g., discipline referrals), and participant (teacher, administrator) satisfaction surveys earned generally positive evaluations from school staff. Results for children were most often related specifically to reductions in office referrals for discipline problems. Evaluations completed more recently have continued to demonstrate positive and more expansive effects for EBS initiatives in both elementary and secondary schools (Bohannon, 2006). For example, evaluation research in one middle school (Metzler et al., 2001) demonstrated that when an EBS program was effectively implemented, positive reinforcement by teachers for appropriate social behavior increased, and aggressive social behavior by students decreased. Students' perceptions of school safety improved at the target school but did not change at comparison schools. Students at the target school reported being less frequently victimized by aggression and felt safer in the hallways and cafeteria. Discipline referrals decreased significantly for seventh graders, and referrals for peer harassment decreased for all male students. In sum, the accumulating research to date indicates that programs that are designed to address the context in which student behavior takes place can be highly successful in reducing negative student behavior and increasing positive behavior (Sprague & Walker, 2005).

An Overlooked Setting: The School Bus

Undoubtedly the school bus is the most poorly understood social context in the school, yet it is a context in which a surprising amount of aggressive behavior is reported. The school bus is an extension of the school in that it provides transportation explicitly authorized and supervised by the school. It is also commonly recognized among school staff, students, and parents as a setting where aggressive acting-out behavior is more common that the larger population might imagine. As a result, aggressive, disruptive behavior on the school bus is a major concern for school administrators, even though the general population may not be aware of it.

While training in child behavior or child development is usually not required of school bus drivers as a condition of employment, drivers are often responsible for twice as many students as classroom teachers are. Perhaps more important, drivers cannot, for reasons of safety, give their full attention to student behavior while they are driving. Thus, aggression on the school bus is potentially more dangerous to more students than in any other school context and should be an element of a comprehensive schoolwide effort to improve the social climate and reduce problem behavior.

Programs of positive behavior and climate change on school buses typically comprise three distinct elements: training for drivers, appropriate policies in the school, and consequences for students. Many school districts provide training in student management for their bus drivers (Vail, 1997). Training typically gives drivers the verbal strategies to present expectations, explain consequences, and control aggressive and disruptive behavior without becoming punitive, hostile, or aggressive.

A variety of school policies have been studied in the past two decades, again with some consistent results. A number of districts have instituted supervised loading zones, which provide a calming influence on students and reinforce rules for safe behavior as they leave school and enter the bus (Tucker, Petrie & Lindauer, 1998). As in classrooms and schools, clear consistent rules that are fairly enforced seem to reduce aggressive behavior on the school bus. The most successful policies are those that align rules in the bus with rules in the school and classroom; school bus rules should place particular emphasis on the need for students to remain seated at all times. Further, schools that recognize drivers as a part of the educational mission and treat their drivers with respect and professionalism seem to benefit from improved civility on the bus as well as in the school.

Another effective school policy, specific agreements signed by students and their parents to obey school bus rules, relates to the third element of a school bus program: consequences. Students should know that aggression will be dealt with swiftly, and the specific consequences of aggression should be spelled out clearly (Tucker, Petrie & Lindauer, 1998). The most effective consequences are those that are invoked within twenty-four hours or no more than forty-eight hours after the problem behavior. One very effective consequence is the immediate loss of riding privileges, which typically requires parent contact. When parents are inconvenienced by having to supply alternative transportation, they typically join with the school to improve student behavior. Equally important, when students lose riding privileges, they lose an important time for socializing with other students. Another novel and effective strategy used by some school districts is providing students with immediate rewards for positive behaviors (Green, Bailey & Barber, 1981). Schools have provided student-requested music on buses, raffles for passes to movie theaters, and fast-food coupons where student behavior on buses reached a certain standard for a specified number of days or weeks.

As I have said, the BrainPower Program is a focused program of aggression reduction that will be most effective when it is used along with comprehensive strategies to support positive behaviors and decrease negative behaviors. A number of strategies and formal programs are available to address behavior problems in schools, and, as we have seen, the success of some has been well documented. The school is the most obvious location for such childhood aggression reduction programs because children are gathered together there, are likely to enact aggression in school settings, and can easily be reached for intervention programs. However, the universally agreed upon unit for childhood socialization is the family. Therefore, we turn next to a consideration of childhood aggression and its reduction in the context of the family.

CHAPTER 6

Childhood Aggression in the Family and the Community

Most of us would agree that the family has the primary responsibility for teaching children to be appropriate in their social behavior. Not surprisingly, there has been a great deal of interest in the characteristics of families that seem to predict whether children are aggressive. As a result, we now have a reasonably clear picture of how children's aggression can be influenced by a number of family characteristics, including family relations and environmental circumstances. A child's behavior is influenced by both individual and environmental factors, and a family's impact on the child's behavior results from a combination of individual and environmental factors. Not only the individual family members and their interactions but also the context in which the family must function have strong influences on a child's behavior. Since parents are generally the primary agents of a child's socialization within the family, we should expect parents' (or primary caregivers') behavior to be very influential in the development of children's aggression. In fact, that expectation has been borne out in a number of studies. In addition to the intuitive and well-researched findings about the importance of parents' personal behavior, including drug use, criminality, and spousal abuse, there are findings that strongly implicate the behavior parents direct toward their children in the development of aggression. The two kinds of parenting behaviors that have received the greatest attention are parental discipline and the quality of the parent-child relationship.

Parental Discipline

One influence of parental discipline has been carefully documented over the past three decades by Gerald Patterson and his colleagues (Reid, Patterson & Snyder, 2002). This work has demonstrated a kind of training that occurs as a result of particular disciplinary practices. At the heart of their findings is a connection between parental discipline and child behavior—specifically, that ineffective parental discipline is a powerful way to teach children that aggressive behavior is a successful social strategy. For example, a parent may issue direct instructions, a request, or a command to a young child. If the child does not comply, the exchange may escalate into a heated and then an aggressive exchange (e.g., yelling, a tantrum, threats, hitting—including the child striking the parent). If that increase in aggressive behavior ultimately causes the parent to give in to the child's demands, the child is rewarded for aggressive behavior. Children who use aggressive tactics to successfully turn back their parents' attempts at behavioral control are likely over time to repeat and strengthen rather than reduce the aggression.

Consider the scene in a typically harried household with two working parents and three school-age children. One parent may be preparing dinner in the kitchen while the other parent straightens up the mess left from the morning's hurried exodus from the house for work and school. A major dispute erupts over the one television set; a ten-year-old physically hits and pushes a seven-year-old to wrest control of the television remote and change the channel. The seven-year-old responds by kicking the older child and yelling for help from the parents. When the parent in the kitchen responds to the yells with "Alex, don't tease your little brother or you're in big trouble," the older child grabs the younger child in a headlock and screams, "I'm gonna smash him; he stole the remote." The parent, apparently abandoning the directive to the older child, then says loudly, "OK, OK, watch whatever you want; dinner is in fifteen minutes." Both children have learned a significant lesson. The older sibling is refining aggressive tactics that successfully achieve personal goals, while the younger child has learned that the more aggressive the behavior, the greater the likelihood of success.

This simple example describes how early aggressive outbursts might, over time, actually train young children in how best to use such behavior to accomplish their own goals. This kind of family interaction is often referred to as a coercive cycle: the parent responds to negative behavior with a command; the child responds by increasing the aggression; the parent increases the level of aggression; eventually the parent withdraws the demand. In this cycle, the child's behavior is reinforced when the parent eventually withdraws the demand, in a process known as negative reinforcement. (That is, the negative experience or event is removed from the child's environment. In this example the parent's threat of discipline is removed.) The parent's behavior is also negatively reinforced, because by capitulating to the child, the child's aggression ends for the moment. Although the parent's strategy may be ineffective in reducing aggression, both the child and the parent are rewarded. The hallmarks of family interaction that develop a child's aggression are (1) the gradual extension of the length of time for a coercive episode, (2) a progressive increase in anger, hostility, aggression, and generally noxious behaviors by all parties, and (3) the eventual withdrawal of the parent (or sibling) from interaction with the child who is aggressive.

Our example also points to the role of siblings in coercive cycles of behavior. Social interactions among brothers and sisters can provide important training for aggressive behavior and may be more influential than parent interaction in training for physical aggression. Once siblings get into a coercive cycle, the children are up to five times more likely to hit a sibling than a parent. This is understandable, because children have a relatively equal status in the household, and during childhood hitting a brother or sister may be a less risky option than hitting a more powerful (physically, emotionally, and organizationally) parent. However, whether the physical aggression occurs between siblings or between parents and children, the behavior is a strong predictor of the children's violent delinquency once they reach adolescence. Over time, as cycles of aggressive behavior with parents, brothers, and sisters become established patterns of family interaction, the highly aggressive child develops the ability to control family members through aggression. Small wonder that such children take aggressive behavior into subsequent interactions with others: they have learned early in life that aggression is a successful strategy for controlling relationships with others.

However, the links between a family's coercive interactions and a child's aggression may be a bit different for girls than for boys (Zahn-Waxler & Polanichka, 2004). As we have seen, families with high rates of coercive and aggressive interactions have children, both boys and girls, who are aggressive. Over the elementary school years such interactions sometimes increase aggressive behavior, but research finds different patterns for boys and girls. More research has been done with boys who are highly aggressive, showing that they consistently become even more aggressive over time. In contrast, girls' levels of aggressive behavior may remain stable, may mirror changes in boys' behavior, or may even increase at rates greater than boys' (Bierman et al., 2004). One possible explanation of this greater variation in effects on girls' behavior has been girls' greater receptivity to adult socialization. Girls may be more responsive to parental anger than boys are, which may reduce girls' inclination to prolong and intensify the coercive cycles. Also, girls may be more responsive than boys to positive messages from parents, such as emotional rewards for showing prosocial behavior, and may therefore be less likely to increase their aggression during childhood. However, some research suggests that attachment to the home environment is stronger for girls than for boys in childhood and adolescence, making stress and conflict in the home a greater influence on girls' behavior and emotional well-being than is true for boys (Loeber & Stouthamer-Loeber, 1986).

Another feature of parental discipline related to childhood aggression is the timing and type of disciplinary action. In the scenario described above, the parent might at different times withdraw the demand for the child to stop, ignore the children's shouts altogether, issue a vague threat, or come into the living room and somehow verbally or physically discipline the older child. If a parent does not make sure that there are consistent consequences blocking a child's ability to succeed with aggressive tactics when they occur in the home, children will quickly learn that aggression works at least some of the time, and they are likely to repeat the behavior with the expectation of at least occasional success. A parent's pattern of inconsistent responses would be labeled by those who study general principles of human behavior as examples of intermittent reinforcement (Thorpe & Olsen, 1990)—reinforcement that happens sometimes, but not all the time, for a particular behavior. Research has demonstrated repeatedly that intermittent reinforcement is the most powerful means of ensuring that a behavior will persist and . possibly increase. A person whose behavior is sometimes reinforced will ever more optimistically pursue the given behavior in anticipation of the desired reward. If the expected reward is not forthcoming in one instance, the human tendency is to continue the behavior in pursuit of the expected reward. When children who are aggressive sometimes succeed in forcing other family members to withdraw a demand or behavior, they are likely to repeat their behavior with the expectation that eventually they will be successful again.

On the other hand, when the parent persists with efforts at discipline but the verbal discipline is vague, then the child will be likely to ignore the parent altogether. Parental communications or commands to a child in a discipline episode can vary from clear, explicit directions to start or stop a specific behavior to vague statements that are not clearly related to the situation at hand (McMahon & Forehand, 2003). Remember our sibling fight over the television set? The parent's first command was to "stop teasing," but it is not clear that either child was teasing. Rather, the older child hit, and the younger child responded in kind. A clear, direct command to both children would be a specific statement to "stop hitting immediately." The consequence that the parent offered was "big trouble"; a clear, direct consequence would be "turn off the TV" or perhaps, for the instigator of the struggle, "go to your room." Nevertheless, even if the parental directives are clear, the parent must remain engaged to be sure that the children are responsive to the commands and, if not, that the consequences are enforced. Clear communication is important but not enough; follow-through and consistency are perhaps the most important elements of discipline that can deter children from escalating their aggressive behavior.

However, most people now generally understand that physically harsh parental discipline, consistent or not, is no better at reducing or stopping aggression in children than is parental acquiescence or inconsistency. Martin Hoffman (2000) has developed a theory of discipline strategies that helps explain the connection between harsh discipline and childhood aggression. What he refers to as "power-assertive discipline" (physical punishment, threats, humiliation) is strongly associated with aggressive behavior in children. A different discipline strategy, "induction" (explaining to children how their aggressive behavior has harmed others), is linked to children's helping behavior, concern for victims, and the internalization of parents' moral values. When children are threatened with harm or actually harmed, they focus more on the punishment they receive than on their own aggressive behavior and its consequences to the victim. As with a coercive cycle, an exclusive reliance on power-assertive discipline teaches children that aggressive behavior is controlled by those who are more powerful. But if children are to learn to self-regulate behavior in the absence of powerful adult authority, they must understand that aggression is harmful to others and morally wrong. That understanding comes, according to Hoffman, in the exchange between parent and child when discipline must be administered. Inductive explanations teach children by using their behavior as an example of the harm that can be caused. Harsh, physical, power-assertive tactics, rather than teaching that aggression causes harm, actually teach children that aggression can be quite useful and that the powerful authority figure who models such behaviors is someone to be emulated.

The relationship between harsh physical discipline and childhood aggression must be qualified by several situational factors (Repetti, Taylor & Seeman, 2002; Van Leeuwen et al., 2004). A parent's power-assertive discipline tactics have more influence on the development of aggression in grade-school children and adolescents than in toddlers and preschoolers. As with the coercive exchanges described earlier, harsh parental discipline is sometimes more likely to increase aggressive behavior in boys than in girls. Moreover, a mother's harsh discipline is more closely linked to escalation in childhood aggression than is a father's discipline. Overall, harsh discipline is most likely to increase childhood aggressive behavior when it is administered by mothers to their preadolescent or adolescent sons. An aggressive mother-son interaction may tend to increase the development of aggression in boys more than an aggressive mother-daughter interaction tends to increase the development of aggression in girls because mothers spend more time than fathers in caregiving activities with children and because girls are sometimes likely to respond to harsh treatment by internalizing problems (e.g., depression, avoidant attitudes; Repetti, Taylor & Seeman, 2002).

We also now know that the link between discipline and aggressive behavior in children is moderated by the emotional quality of the parent-child relationship. The lack of a connection between early physical discipline (short of actual child abuse) and childhood aggression was first identified in African-American families, where research discovered that such discipline was not related to children's aggressive behavior (Deater-Deckard & Dodge, 1997). Subsequent evidence from both cross-cultural comparisons and research in the United States has found that when physical discipline (short of abuse) is normative and acceptable in a community or culture and not an indication of out-of-control or deviant parenting, both parents and children find the strategy to be evidence of positive care rather than hostile, angry parenting (Simons et al., 2002). These findings suggested yet another principle of contextual effects. The broader lesson is the importance of warm parent-child relations as a context for disciplining children, and this is true across all ethnicities (McLoyd & Smith, 2002). Firm, loving control, however defined by cultural and community norms, is an essential ingredient of healthy development for all children.

There also can be a role for power assertion in any discipline encounter in any community. When a child is either so emotionally aroused that they are unlikely to attend to the parent's message or likely to feel vindicated by the aggressive act, some kind of physical intervention might be necessary to get the child to pay attention to the parent's induction. A first grader who has pushed a child off a bike may feel vindicated and excited to claim a turn that they feel was unfairly denied them. If the victim was hurt, the child might neither notice nor care. In such an instance, it might be necessary for the parent to bodily remove the child from the bike to be sure that the child is attending to the message contained in an inductive discipline encounter and recognizes the harm done to the victim.

Parents using strategies to gain a child's attention or control behavior in a discipline episode must be careful to self-regulate their own anger. Power-assertive exchanges, taken to extremes, become abusive punishment. A wealth of research has connected abusive physical punishment (spanking or hitting to cause bruises) with children's aggressive and antisocial behavior, emotional problems, bullying, and poor peer relations in all communities (Moeller, 2001). Parents who strike their children with enough force to leave visible marks or injury, something that typically happens when a parent is angry and out of control, may find that their children become aggressive, less in control of their own emotions, and likely to engage in delinquent acts. Unfortunately, abusive physical punishment is all too often accompanied by emotional abuse; the parent who strikes out physically in anger is also prone to verbally humiliating, threatening, and belittling the child. The combination of physical and emotional abuse delivered by an out-of-control parent has, as we might expect, strong links to childhood aggression.

Carefully documented explorations of those links (Downey et al., 1998; Pearce & Pezzot-Pearce, 2007) indicate that children who experience this kind of harsh punishment look at the world in a defensive manner that makes them hypervigilant and inaccurate in their assessment of aggression in others as well as quick to respond with aggression. This kind of punishment seems to be one of the ways that the pattern of overestimating harmful intent in others, described in Chapter 2 as a hostile attributional bias, is established in children (Dodge, Petit & Bates, 1997). The presence of this level of family aggression, or abuse, is also a very clear signal that the family's functioning, beyond specific discipline tactics, is severely impaired.

Understanding the overall quality of family relationships and functioning, an important influence on children's aggression, is the topic to which we now turn.

The Quality of Family Relationships

Disrupted or dysfunctional family relations can lead to children's aggression. Although dysfunctional family relations certainly include harsh, abusive parenting, such parental discipline tactics are only a part of the dysfunction. Patterns of relations can be very different across families—as different as the many variations in family structures that exist today. But within such variability, some important traits stand out. A well-studied hallmark of the dysfunctional family is domestic violence. Like abusive discipline, marital conflict has been strongly associated with aggression and antisocial behavior in childhood and beyond (Ehrensaft et al., 2003).

Conversely, a well-functioning family is a cooperative and emotionally positive unit. Parents take responsibility for the role of primary caregiver. They consistently set and enforce clear rules of behavior but maintain flexibility to revise rules as needed. Perhaps most important for our discussion, in well-functioning families children feel loved and cared for by parents and are secure in their roles as members of the family. Parents are warm and caring toward children but do not confuse warmth with indulgence; in lavishing love, they do not abandon their responsibility to guide, manage, and monitor their children. A wealth of research has examined the role of parenting in the development of children's competence (Bugental & Grusec, 2006), much of it using a framework of parenting styles first developed by Diana Baumrind (1978). The evidence is clear that parents who apply a combination of emotional warmth and firm control, whatever the normative definitions of those terms may be in a given cultural context, raise children who tend to be socially and emotionally competent, have high internal standards of morality, and display a low propensity for aggressive and violent behavior.

The opposite of parental emotional warmth is often defined as emotional rejection. When children do not feel that parents provide enough nurturance, interest, and involvement, the children are very likely to display some kind of aggression. One explanation for the link between parental emotional rejection and childhood aggression has been offered by attachment theory (Bowlby, 1980). When parents are uncaring and unresponsive to a child's needs, the child may not develop bonds of trust (also known as attachment) with the parents. The absence of this basic human bond, according to some who study attachment theory, leaves the child with a poorly developed conscience (Magid & McKelvey, 1987) and the inability to internalize the parents' values and standards (Cavell, 2000). Over time, the child begins to reject the expectations and values of the emotionally rejecting parents. The parents, in turn, lose their authority to positively reinforce the child when he or she is behaving appropriately.

Instead, attachment theory argues, children of emotionally rejecting parents begin to respond to their seemingly uncaring parents with aggression and anger in an effort to signal their needs and their distress. They also develop an "internal working model," or mental representation, of relationships as untrustworthy, uncaring, and callous. When they take this mental model into their peer group, they anticipate rejection from peers, behave aggressively, and come to be rejected. Emotional rejection, like abusive discipline, typically leads to a hypervigilant expectation of rejection and to the kind of escalating spiral of aggression and peer rejection that is described in Chapter 2.

Emotional rejection is one of a collection of parental behaviors that together are considered neglectful parenting. Neglect is somewhat different from abusive parenting, although abuse and neglect often occur together (Manly et al., 2001). While abuse refers to harmful things that parents do to their children, neglect refers to parental inaction, extraordinary inattentiveness, or other omissions in parenting responsibility that harm or endanger a child's physical or emotional well-being. Neglect implies that parents are not concerned with their children's social activities and friends. Neglect, like emotional rejection, is an indicator of an unresponsive parent and a disrupted parent-child relationship. Conversely, awareness of a child's needs and desires seems to be one of the foundations of skillful parenting. Equally vital, successful parents distinguish between the importance of meeting a child's needs sufficiently for healthy development and the dangers of indulging a child's every whim.

Neglectful parenting has been clearly linked to the development of aggressive behavior in childhood and violent criminal behavior in adolescence and adulthood (Knutson, DeGarmo & Reid, 2004). The processes that link parental neglect to childhood aggression and youthful violence are not completely clear, but research suggests two possible pathways. As with many of the influences discussed in this chapter, neglect seems to influence children's aggression by its impact on relations within the family as well as its impact on the child's environment.

Inside the family and in the child's environment, two specific kinds of neglectful behaviors have been studied by those who are concerned with children's aggression: lack of parental care and lack of proper supervision (Knutson et al., 2005). Lack of parental care typically means the absence of reasonable physical care, including basic hygiene, clean clothing, adequate food, reasonable shelter (e.g., free of vermin and filth), and adequate sleep time. Care neglect may also include highly irregular school attendance (educational neglect), prolonged absences on a parent's part (abandonment), delay or denial of health care (medical neglect), or exposure to drugs or alcohol. Because care neglect covers a range of specific actions that parents omit or commit, research findings have been slow to identify specific links between children's aggressive behavior and parents' care neglect. However, recent research (Knutson, DeGarmo & Reid, 2004; Knutson et al., 2005) is beginning to untangle these relationships. Early findings suggest that children entering first grade who are not receiving adequate physical care are more aggressive in their behavior as reported by parents, teachers, peers, and playground observers. As these young children progress through school, their behavior becomes more aggressive, and they become more rejected by peers. This is equally true for boys and for girls. Children who experience physical neglect relatively later in childhood may also display heightened aggressive behavior, but this kind of neglect does not seem to lead as often to greater increases in aggression or rejection as children enter adolescence. Physical neglect may be a symptom of more general household disruption or parental maladjustment (e.g., substance abuse, mental illness, criminal activity), and the effect of a disordered family on the child depends somewhat on how the child is able to respond. On the one hand, such family instability is more easily escaped by relatively older children. However, relatively older children who are physically neglected may more easily affiliate with deviant peers who do not reject them but join together to form deviant peer groups.

Supervisory neglect, typically defined as inadequate or nonexistent monitoring and supervision of a child's activities and friends, plays a unique but highly related role in the development of children's aggression. Supervisory neglect includes the absence of direct monitoring of a child's activities away from home (e.g., calling to see if a friend's parents are at home when the child is visiting, discussing where children are going and with whom), setting rules for activities at home and away from home, discussing the child's daily activities, engaging in joint activities that allow time for more intimate discussions (e.g., cooking together, sharing hobbies or games), and being aware of school successes and difficulties (in behavior and academics). Some have even argued that parental monitoring is effective because it provides the opportunity for conversation between parents and children, and children will disclose important information if they feel it will be accepted and attended to (Stattin & Kerr, 2000).

Children of inattentive parents may not reap the benefits of positive peer relations as a way to promote social functioning in early childhood because the parents may not be involved in providing adequate social experiences for their children. Such children are less socially competent than they might be with more social experiences in the early years and are thus more likely to be rejected by peers in middle childhood, when children gain some control over their social relations. Children who consistently experience parental neglect are also more likely to befriend deviant peers whose parents are also inattentive. These deviant peer groups are far more likely to engage in delinquent and antisocial behavior in middle childhood and adolescence than are their peers with adequate parental attention. Older children who do not receive active supervision—what we commonly think of as parental guidance and monitoring—are much more likely than supervised children to display aggressive, violent, and antisocial behavior in adolescence. Boys in middle and late childhood are more likely to experience supervisory neglect, perhaps because as they grow older, they are given a certain amount of freedom to roam away from home and adult supervision. However, this increase in freedom can come at a steep price in adolescent antisocial activities.

Parental neglect is, in fact, related to abusive physical punishment as well. In families with poor supervision, boys are especially likely to experience harsh physical discipline, which suggests that in families in disarray, boys are more likely to be poorly monitored and engage in antisocial behavior than are boys in functional families.

Their antisocial behavior leads parents to discipline them with harsh physical discipline, leading to a progressive deterioration of parent-child relations. Although quality of care and supervision are often highly related in the same family, they represent distinct types of parental neglect and have somewhat different effects on children at different ages and of either gender.

The Role of the Environment

It is important to remember that the quality of family functioning is influenced not only by relations within the family but also by the context in which the family must function. For example, child monitoring and supervision can be extremely difficult in communities that do not offer easily accessible, supervised activities for children after school. Rural and newly developed outer suburban communities, though sometimes more affluent or crime free than urban communities, may lack an established infrastructure of community organizations and public transportation that allow children access to safe activities. The burden of providing such supervision then falls onto parents. Parents from across the social spectrum who may already be occupied with demands in the workplace due to high-status employment, long commutes, or long work hours may be unavailable for effective supervision. However, children who are not in safe, supervised activities after school typically have significant increases in aggressive and delinquent behavior over the course of middle childhood and adolescence (Garner, Zhao & Gillingham, 2002). Thus, programs for children in the community can stand in for effective parental supervision and monitoring, with a positive impact on children's behavior.

Although all communities may contain structural risk factors for the development of children's aggression, economically disadvantaged communities are typically burdened by multiple risk factors that have an impact on the development and display of aggression in childhood. Research in both community psychology and sociology tells us that children living in dysfunctional neighborhoods (i.e., characterized by crime, litter and graffiti, substandard housing, easy availability of alcohol and other drugs, and few safe activities) with relatively high rates of community violence more often engage in aggressive behavior than do children living in safer and better resourced neighborhoods (Horn & Trickett, 1998; Lynch, 2003). A wealth of research using U.S. census data has documented that measures of childhood aggression are greater in communities with high poverty, violence, and crime than in relatively more affluent and more advantaged neighborhoods. The relationship between exposure to community stressors and violent behavior is surprisingly strong for girls (Farrell & Bruce, 1997) and especially strong for both boys and girls in middle childhood (Ingoldsby & Shaw, 2002). Some research suggests that girls' aggressive behavior in these stressful communities actually increases over childhood and adolescence, narrowing somewhat the typically wide gap between the rates of aggression in boys and girls. In the face of high levels of community violence, girls become almost as physically aggressive as the boys in those communities.

Middle childhood may be a time of unique vulnerability because children begin to increase the time they spend outside the house and in activities with peers with little direct adult supervision. Yet at the same time children have not fully developed the cognitive coping skills that can help them navigate the disorder around them and cope with the psychological stress of witnessing acts of violence. Those who study human neurobiology also suggest that persistent community violence and disorder may actually initiate a "rewiring" effect on the brain as the brain attempts to adjust to the repeated, random presentation of information demonstrating that the environment is dangerous (Hudley & Novak, 2007). This possible effect of community violence, like harsh parenting and parental rejection, may promote attributional bias in children—the tendency to misunderstand the intentions of others, overestimate the hostility in others, and respond inappropriately with aggression. Children may be especially vulnerable to this neurobiological effect in middle childhood because their brains are still maturing as they begin to venture farther and more often from home and are increasingly exposed to community violence and disorder.

Although the possible neurobiological changes have not been well researched to date, research with elementary school children has made it clear that those who witness comparatively high amounts of violence have higher levels of aggressive behavior and greater confidence in the appropriateness and effectiveness of aggressive tactics in social situations with peers, relative to children in communities with less violence (Schwartz & Proctor, 2000). Children exposed to chronic community violence may also become desensitized to violence and have trouble developing a concern for others, or empathy (Osofsky, 1995). To successfully socialize children in a dysfunctional community, parents must cope successfully with their own fears and traumas while attempting to provide rigorous monitoring as well as emotional and social supports. Community stressors may understandably have a negative influence on parents' mental health, leading to higher levels of psychological distress, particularly in mothers (Belle & Doucet, 2003). As parents attempt to cope with community stressors and socialize their children, they may adopt inconsistent and harshly punitive discipline, with the attendant problems. The normative task of child socialization may thus become an overwhelming burden for families living in objectively dangerous communities.

Communities in disarray are also likely to be home to residents with few economic resources. The task of child socialization is daunting for impoverished families. The pressure of parenting with limited financial and emotional resources, whether because of chronic or sudden unemployment, underemployment, single-parent status, limited social support systems, or health problems and the associated, often catastrophic uninsured medical expenses, can also contribute significantly to children's aggression when these pressures compromise parents' mental and emotional well-being. Impoverished families, although they may change residences frequently, are financially unable to move from distressed neighborhoods and thus must cope with street crime, substandard housing, inadequate community resources (e.g. no supermarkets with quality food, no safe activities for children), limited employment opportunities, constantly changing neighbors, and poor schools. The combined stress of financial disadvantage and community danger with little hope of escape may lead to problems not only with mental but also with physical health among parents, which can, in turn, compromise parents' ability to effectively socialize and monitor their children. Impoverished parents in distressed communities also often mistrust their often unknown neighbors and are prone to expect negative responses and attitudes from these neighbors. Their modeling of hostile expectations may be yet another source of attributional bias in their children. Parental hostile attributions also contribute to a lack in these communities of a cohesive neighborhood social network that promotes a concern for the well-being of the neighborhood and provides a measure of social control for children. Without these kinds of informal controls, children may come to think that aggression is unlikely to meet with disapproval, and may therefore view it as an acceptable social tactic.

Some research (Sampson, Raudenbush & Earls, 1997) suggests that mutual trust, shared prosocial values, and community solidarity, also known as collective efficacy, can be a strong deterrent to childhood aggression and violence in communities that experience economic hardship and social neglect. Such collective efficacy has emotional benefits for adults, because they achieve a sense of control over their circumstances. For children and youths, some suggest that perceived support from other adults in the neighborhood (including teachers), rather than perceived or actual neighborhood danger, affects psychological well-being and reduces feelings of anger, fear, and isolation (Bowen & Chapman, 1996). In a similar manner within the family, parental emotional support and strict supervision may buffer boys against the negative effects of community violence, but the effects of parental support and supervision for girls may be more indirect (Brookmeyer, Henrich & Schwab-Stone, 2005). Girls seem to benefit from having positive attitudes toward peers, often a characteristic of girls who are socially skilled. Strong social skills, however, may be the result of positive parental socialization.

The Peer Group

Peers play an important role in the development of children's aggression. While we all understand the family to be chiefly responsible for socializing children, the influence of peers increases as children become older, venture out independently to school and into the wider world, and increasingly interact with other children without direct supervision. As described in an earlier chapter, children's aggression sometimes leads to rejection by peers in middle childhood, and that combination of aggression and rejection is especially likely to lead to adjustment and behavioral problems in later life. Rejected children lack the opportunities to learn and refine skills that help them become successful members of social and friendship groups.

However, there is another side to peers and aggression that reflects the power of the peer group with whom children associate. Children who are aggressive tend to be liked by and to like other aggressive children. In fact, aggressive children who become rejected by their more socially appropriate peers tend to seek out more aggressive peers for social interaction. Most important, children (both boys and girls) who are rejected and initially physically aggressive may become even more aggressive over time as they befriend and interact with more aggressive children (Werner & Crick, 2004). In a process known as deviancy training, aggressive children reinforce one another's behavioral aggression and beliefs about aggression in the context of the peer group (Snyder et al., 2005). Aggressive peer groups teach and encourage increasingly aggressive tactics for their members and provide social rewards (e.g., words of encouragement, laughter) and social pressures for the behaviors. Aggressive peer groups can subsequently progress to a broad range of antisocial behaviors in adolescence and beyond, including violent delinquency and criminality, drug use, and risky sexual behavior. Neighborhood peer groups are more likely to have a mix of ages than are school peer groups, whose members tend to come from the same grade or class. Older children who are aggressive may provide training for younger children, making them especially risky companions for children in early elementary school (Ingoldsby & Shaw, 2002). Similarly, older siblings who are already affiliated with aggressive peer groups are a compelling source of deviancy training.

Children develop social connections and friendships with other children who are accessible at school, in the neighborhood, or in organized activities (e.g., sports teams, youth groups, church choirs). Clearly, children's access to peers is regulated by family resources and activities. Parents, by virtue of income and employment, determine where children live. Neighborhoods, in turn, determine where they attend school and what kinds of organized activities are available to them, either in the neighborhood or at school. Impoverished, distressed neighborhoods are home to more than their share of children who are aggressive and fewer than their share of youth activities (Scouts, sports leagues, hobby clubs). Without organized activities that are supervised by adults, children spend more unsupervised time with peers as they grow older and become more independent.

Because larger numbers of children who are highly aggressive live in distressed neighborhoods, living in the midst of community disorder and poverty increases the chances that less aggressive children, both boys and girls, will spend time with more aggressive peers outside the view of adults. Children in distressed communities may have restricted choices for friends, particularly in middle childhood, and may have to choose between solitary activities or peers in the immediate neighborhood and school. Some (but not all) of these peers may be highly aggressive and, particularly if they are older, attempt to exert pressure on other children to conform to expectations for aggressive behavior. Peer pressure to behave aggressively is similarly present in advantaged communities, where parents may be focused on the pressures attendant upon high-status social or professional positions. Children in advantaged communities may also have resources (e.g. disposable income) to support certain antisocial activities. In sum, peers and siblings can function as potent channels for external influences such as a disorganized neighborhood, violence in the community, and peer group expectations. The combination of environment and peers plays a considerable role in shaping the development of aggression in individual children.

Family and Community Intervention

Given that the family and the community are such important influences in the development of children's aggression, it is not surprising that a number of interventions have been developed to focus on family functioning and to address the community context. Parent-centered intervention programs, often offered in connection with school-based programs for behavior change, focus on some combination of management skills, family functioning, and personal problems that interfere with successful parenting. Intervention programs that address management skills typically teach strategies to effectively reduce children's aggression and noncompliance and often teach parents to minimize their own problematic and ineffective parenting behaviors.

For example, Parent Management Training (PMT), one of the more widely used parent-intervention models in school-based programs, teaches parents to promote positive behavior and suppress aggression by changing the way they discipline and reinforce their children's behavior (Christenson, Hirsch & Hurley, 1997; Kazdin, 2005)). Parents learn to identify and track problematic behaviors, to accurately communicate their expectations to children, to establish and enforce appropriate consequences for aggression, and to positively reinforce positive behavior. This intervention strategy is based on the assumption that aggressive behavior is learned in family interactions and that parents of children who are aggressive have the kinds of deficits in parenting skills that were described earlier in this chapter. The intervention focuses explicitly on the interpersonal interaction between parent and child in the home and is typically implemented by a therapist in sessions with a parent over several months. Although research suggests that training parents can decrease children's aggression, program effectiveness is limited when interventions do not also address the quality of family relations or the personal problems that parents may face (Eamon & Venkataraman, 2003).

Some interventions work to change all of the systems in which a child is embedded rather than simply the parent-child interaction, including the full range of family, school, and community systems that define a child's life circumstances. These broad interventions are often more effective than tailored programs precisely because they are more comprehensive and recognize that children's aggressive behavior is the result of influences from a multitude of sources. A number of family-system interventions and family-school collaboration models, including Prosocial Family Therapy (Blechman &

Vryan, 2000), structural family therapy (Minuchin & Fishman, 1981), the FAST program (McDonald, Billingham & Conrad, 1997), and the Fast Track program (Conduct Problems Prevention Research Group, 2002), are based on the understanding that children cannot be helped without addressing the systems that control behavior. A family is an interdependent social system that contains defined subsystems. Within the larger family system, siblings, husband and wife together, and each individual parent and child represent distinct subsystems. Each of these systems and subsystems in the family has a unique influence on children's aggression. Our harried parent in the opening scenario may also be a wife who angrily resents her husband's lack of warmth and support. The brothers may harbor mutual anger from negative exchanges at school or in the neighborhood. The father and older son may have a cold and distant relationship stemming from the child's discovery of the father's infidelity, while the younger son may be the only family member to enjoy a warm relationship with the father. The family system may be so dysfunctional that children may behave aggressively at school as a reaction to problematic interactions at home. Alternatively, the family system may be so disconnected, the members so disengaged, that children receive little or no support, guidance, or even monitoring.

Family systems may be dysfunctional or disconnected for a host of reasons that range far beyond parental management skills. Parental problems like marital discord and violence, substance use, and impaired mental health make strong contributions to children's aggression and must therefore be dealt with in a program of intervention. Aggressive and delinquent siblings are also a part of the family system that can contribute to the target child's aggression. To promote competence throughout the full family system, comprehensive family intervention programs typically add components that teach all family members to use effective communication strategies in all of the family's subsystems as well as with important others (teachers, parents of children's friends). Family problem solving is another important skill often targeted in comprehensive family interventions that relates to effective communication. Families learn to work together in a positive way to resolve problems in the family system as each member works to accommodate his or her behavior within the family, clearly communicates his or her perspective, acknowledges the perspectives of other members, and puts limits on blaming other family members.

Finally, family systems interventions typically address the important skills of monitoring child behavior in the community outside the home. Comprehensive interventions typically teach parents to work collaboratively rather than in confrontation with children and spouses to keep track of what children are doing and where and with whom they are doing it. In particular, parents learn the value of a support network that includes the parents of their children's friends; at the same time, they learn the social and communication skills necessary to develop and maintain these relationships. In distressed neighborhoods, close supervision and behavior management by a network of supportive parents are especially important in interfering with the formation of deviant peer groups and minimizing their impact on younger and more vulnerable children. Learning extends beyond the social community to the school; both parents and children learn the significance of frequent, positive communication with the children's schools and teachers to identify potential problems early and reinforce desirable behaviors and attitudes. Some comprehensive school partnership programs specifically target the school as a social system by helping children develop social competence with peers and providing training for teachers in classroom management and home-school communication.

Overall, comprehensive intervention programs have positive effects on parents' personal behavior and family management, family functioning, children's school performance, and children's behavior. These programs, by simultaneously targeting child behavior, family interaction, and family-school-community connections, provide the greatest gains for children who are aggressive and their families, compared with programs that target a single aspect of aggression. Interventions that recognize the multiple influences that shape aggressive behavior and work to improve all of the systems in a child's life (family, school peers, community) are the best and strongest complement to programs that help children improve their individual behavior. Given the weight of evidence in favor of programs of comprehensive support for children, their families, their schools, and their communities, it is reasonable to think about the kinds of social policies that could provide a level of support necessary for the healthy development of all children. We turn next to a consideration of public policy and its impact on the development of childhood aggression.

CHAPTER 7

Public Policy for Children's Well-Being

As we have seen, the development of aggression in childhood is influenced by a range of factors including an individual child's perceptions of the world; the child's family circumstances; the child's school; and the larger community, society, and culture in which the child is positioned. The BrainPower Program has shown that children's perceptions can be changed and that changing the perceptions of aggressive children can lead to improvements in their behavior. However, as effective as the program might be, children's aggression is much more than an individual behavioral problem. Therefore, I have also discussed strategies and programs for families, schools, and communities that might have a positive impact on childhood aggression while promoting optimal youth development. Is it not prudent now to wonder why, given a reasonable accumulation of knowledge, our families, schools, and communities are not more successful in supporting the development of positive rather than aggressive behavior in more of our children? What will it take to apply our knowledge to the lives of real children and families in real schools and communities? For an answer to those questions, let us turn to a discussion of policy initiatives that might support the widespread application of scientific knowledge to reduce aggression and enhance the well-being of all children. Because, as Pittman and Irby (1996) have wisely noted, "Problem free is not fully prepared," this selective discussion will pay special attention to policies that build on the strengths of children, families, schools, and communities.

A unifying theme of this book is the idea that when children feel threatened, they are likely to act with aggression, whether or not the threat is real. Children must feel safe, cared for, and secure to attain their most positive developmental outcomes. Policies should be in place that support efforts by all of the important people in a child's life, including the child, to establish the feeling of comfort and security necessary for healthy development. In this chapter I will highlight policy initiatives that might minimize the development of aggressive behavior and support positive development for all children. Although the universe of policies that can improve the health and welfare of children is very large, the discussion here will focus tightly on policies that might support children, their communities, their families, and their schools in efforts to reduce children's aggressive behavior by providing them with a sense of safety and security.

The Neighborhood

The previous chapter offered a compelling picture of the multiple ways in which communities can influence the development of children's aggression. Recall that communities in disarray, which typically includes economic disadvantage, poor resources, high rates of violence and crime, deviant peers, and substandard housing, provide an especially fertile ground for the development of childhood aggression. Families who are forced by economic or social circumstances to settle in such communities are likely to find their children vulnerable to the development of aggressive and antisocial behavior. Well-established public policies in urban centers have dismantled concentrated residential poverty by distributing small numbers of public housing units across middle-income neighborhoods or by providing low-income families with housing subsidies that allow them to live in available housing in middle-income neighborhoods. Low-income public housing that is organized into high-rise apartments or separated "compounds" concentrates poverty and its negative consequences very effectively. Distributed models of housing, on the other hand, benefit families and children by decreasing the possibility that they will have to live in dysfunctional communities.

Public policy that places poor families in safer, better-resourced, and more functional communities can provide parents with additional support to manage children's activities and shield vulnerable children from community violence. Family support may take the form of supervised activity programs, good transportation services, and the absence of violent criminal co-residents in the neighborhood. Stable communities also provide support to parents in the form of networks with other attentive and engaged parents. This resource of relationships, or social capital, can successfully work against the development of children's aggression. As described in the previous chapter, parents who work together can provide more effective social control for children and adolescents than parents working alone can. Research on neighborhood characteristics (Bould, 2003) suggests that attentive neighbors can provide a collective set of eyes to monitor children and interrupt aggressive and disruptive behavior in its early stages. However, public policy that concentrates poor urban families into impoverished, distrustful communities may leave families and their children very much adrift; in such neighborhoods even the full weight of the law (e.g., response times for a 911 call) may not be available to interrupt antisocial behavior. Although evidence is mounting that childhood aggression can be significantly influenced by housing policies, these effects have been documented mainly in urban centers. Rural communities that comprise concentrations of families living in poverty, though different in character from urban centers, also experience disarray. Public policy responses to block the negative impacts of rural concentrated poverty often leave families and children vulnerable but invisible in isolated rural communities. However, providing excellent educational opportunities, job training and opportunities for families, and meaningful activities for children and youths (e.g., community service, after-school programs, work experiences) are all strategies for combating poverty and hopelessness that should work equally well for residents in all communities. For example, isolated rural communities might benefit greatly from policies that bring Internet access to provide distance learning and telecommuting opportunities.

Whatever people's economic and geographic circumstances, residents of a community must work together—exhibit collective efficacy—to support the positive development of their children. Social policy can support parents in these efforts in many ways. Over the past two decades, a substantial body of information has been produced that can inform community efforts to support children's positive development. Starting from a framework, first synthesized by the Search Institute (Benson, 1990), that describes developmental assets, research has now begun to specify the characteristics of what are called developmentally attentive communities (Benson, 1997; Lerner and Benson, 2003) and the policies that might foster such communities. Such communities and policies concentrate on building children's strengths by valuing and encouraging their voices and competencies, offering clear boundaries and expectations, and providing meaningful activities that connect them to community service. As we have already discussed, opportunities to build prosocial skills and behaviors in after-school enrichment programs that develop children's talents and creativity (dance classes, video production projects, poetry "slams"), do much more to reduce childhood aggression than do punitive school or policing policies.

How can policy be marshaled in support of communities and their children? First and foremost, communities must learn how to advocate on their own behalf. Because community needs vary widely across a broad array of indicators, including socioeconomic status, location (e.g., rural, urban, suburban), and ethnic makeup, it is difficult to formulate with certainty general policies and programs that work for all communities. Some very specific policies that affect children's behavior in school and after school, as well as those that affect parents' capacities to parent their children, are discussed below. However, I want to begin this discussion of specific policy at the level of community efficacy, because residents themselves can be uniquely situated to identify relevant policy initiatives yet are at times the only group that is completely shut out of decisionmaking. Community empowerment initiatives presume that community residents have at least as much to bring to the conversation as professional staff and political leaders do and that change can be effected without constructing new centralized agencies with outside staff to implement new programs targeting a specific category of child (e.g., adolescent offenders) or outcome (e.g., reduce antisocial behavior between 3 and 6 p.m.). Rather, empowered communities work collaboratively with their own members and the larger political structure to maximize positive developmental outcomes for all children and all residents. Policymakers must therefore adopt as their own policy the idea of empowering communities to collaborate on the shaping and implementation of policy.

Community empowerment initiatives must recognize twin foci: the will (Do I want to get involved with this issue?) and the capacity (Am I able to work for change, and do I know what to do?) of families and other residents, schools, community organizations, faith congregations, and businesses to participate in discussion and action on behalf of the neighborhood's children (Granger, 2002). The first step for any program of community empowerment should be a community needs assessment, for which community members come together to discuss particular issues, concerns, and community needs. Public entities (states, cities, etc.) that are committed to community empowerment as an article of policy must recognize that resources, both financial resources and professional technical assistance, must be allocated to support the process. A thoughtful, collaborative assessment should highlight the state of community will and community capacity to manage change.

Various policies can build the community's will. For example, altering contingencies for action can lead to enhanced participation. A private or governmental employer could offer paid time off for employees to participate in a planned mentoring program for community youths, and a private employer might receive tax incentives for providing these in-kind resources to the local community. Perhaps a neighbor-to-neighbor campaign might be necessary for raising awareness about a need for change and collective action to effectively support youth in the community. As a general rule, most people feel more comfortable learning from and working with familiar or at least recognizable members of their community, not strangers, so a campaign of persuasion or information dissemination to raise community members' will for collective action is probably best conducted by known people.

Community capacity building has also been the goal of a variety of public policy initiatives. For example, the federal initiative supporting community Weed and Seed programs to reduce youth antisocial behavior and violence has been renamed the Community Capacity Development Office in recognition of the need to empower communities to help themselves. Leadership development and training in community organizing remain important strategies for community capacity building. Community economic development is also often a central need in low-income communities that suffer disproportionately from childhood antisocial behavior. Leadership development might require a policy that targets individuals, such as an income tax credit for families of modest means who are saving to send children to college, free or low-cost education services to increase parents' earning potential, or a childcare tax credit that recognizes the need for services through elementary school. Policy at the neighborhood level might be a variant of the familiar neighborhood empowerment zones that provide tax incentives for businesses if they are willing to locate in a particular neighborhood and provide opportunities for employment to residents, including youths. Government at all levels might also embrace policies that represent a direct investment in children and youths, including resources for facilities (new or improved schools and community centers), programs (staffed recreation programs, extended library hours), and opportunities (youth intern programs with business and government). Although empowered communities might concentrate on any number of specific actions on behalf of children, I will now turn to a discussion of a common core of policies that represent what is best for all children, both in and out of school, and their families.

The After-School Hours

As we have seen in an earlier chapter, how children spend their time has a great deal to do with the development of aggressive behavior. A number of both government and academic research reports have demonstrated the potential dangers for children who are left without safe, supervised activities after school. Therefore, our national discussion about day-care quality and child success should be extended beyond the current focus on toddlers and preschoolers to consider the quality of care we provide for both children and adolescents during nonschool hours. All families, and especially those families with an economic disadvantage, would benefit as much from well-planned after-school care for children in middle childhood as they do from high-quality early-childhood programs, with their proven benefits (Vandell & Wolfe, 2000). Our thinking in this area must be broadened to include the full breadth of childhood and adolescence in policy debate and development.

The problems generated by too little parental monitoring as well as the stress placed on working parents who struggle to manage their children's unsupervised after-school hours, often via telephone, could be minimized substantially with high-quality after-school programs. If supervised after-school activities enhance children's appropriate behavior, reduce juvenile crime and violence, and support healthy development, all children should have access to such programs. I am reminded of a conversation, not too many years ago, with a fourth grader, Keith, who was rated by his teacher as quite aggressive before participation in the BrainPower Program. He was parented by single, wage-earning mother who stayed in touch with her children by phone after school hours. Keith described his life during the hours after school, which were spent primarily with a tightly knit group who went to the same neighborhood school and lived in apartment buildings on the same block. The three male friends walked to school together, played together at recess and lunchtime, walked home together, and spent time together during evenings and weekends. Keith and his friends played at the local park, rode their bikes around a restricted area of the neighborhood, visited at one another's homes, and played video games at home. There was no formal after-school program at his school, and the single staff person at the community park was responsible only for grounds maintenance.

Although Keith did not offer any descriptions of conflicts or aggression within his set of peers and although his teacher's rating of his reactive aggression showed a marked decline after participation in the BrainPower Program, violence and aggression seemed to be a fact of life for these children. Apparently they did not often feel safe at the local park in the evening hours because "gangbangers are in there at certain times, smoking crack and acting wild. They take our balls and our stuff if they catch us." Keith said that during weekday evenings, he rarely played outside on his own block. On the weekends, when these friends ventured out to the park, they always rode bikes so that if "gangbangers are there and they try to bother us, we just ride straight at them like we're going to run over them. Then we keep riding until we're long gone."

Clearly, the behavior of some highly aggressive children is shaped in significant ways by their social environment, and that behavior can be quite amenable to change. Keith's description of his life shows the need for an environment that provides safe after-school activities. Creative public policies might expand our thinking about out-of-school programs that might cover the public park that he finds unsafe much of the time, the possibly underutilized and certainly underfunded public library, and other public services that already exist and could provide enrichment programming after school for children of all ages. Such institutions and agencies (e.g., park services, local museums, libraries) should be central members of discussions and planning groups for youth services at the city, state, and federal level. Resources should be made available for programming for children and youths, and communities and parents should be aware of program availability through the production of resource guides mailed directly to families.

However, a broader policy discussion must include issues of access. We know that parks, museums, and even libraries are not equitably distributed across neighborhoods, and some children's access to these resources is therefore constrained by location and transportation. The allocation of resources to increase library hours, provide staffing for community parks, or build new facilities (e.g., libraries, museums, parks, recreation centers) should be driven in large part by the need to provide healthy communities for all children and youths. Even where facilities (parks, libraries) are present, funds for designated after-school services are especially vulnerable when government budgets are stretched. For example, the 21st Century Community Learning Centers Program, begun in the Clinton administration with $40 million in 1998, supports after-school programs in more than 7,500 public schools across the country, at an estimated cost of nearly $1 billion in 2002. As government revenues wane, support from both federal and matching state and local funds for after-school programs becomes an easy target for elimination because those who benefit most from public programs are among the least powerful in society. Programs in communities across the country are being forced to scale back or close, and families looking for a safe haven for their children are being left behind. Both children ("I get help with my homework; I eat; we do art and card games, dance club and kick ball. And it's just really, really fun") and their parents ("We can't afford day care. I honestly don't know what we'd do without this") across the country are expressing their need for supervised activities during the hours when children are most likely to commit or fall victim to crimes (Magee, 2005). Unmonitored time for youths potentially fosters increased levels of aggressive, antisocial, and delinquent behavior. The consequences for society are far more costly than the price of well-designed after-school programs in easily accessible facilities.

When funding constraints require some services and programs to close, children in some communities may lack access to more-distant programs. Creative public policies might help maintain access. Public transportation policy, which may seem somewhat removed from children's behavior, can have a major impact on a family's access to all kinds of services, including safe, supervised activities. One possible policy is an approach analogous to the policy of transportation support for seniors. If programs cannot be made available to all neighborhoods, children might be transported to existing programs. The cost of transporting children and expanding existing programs might be far below the expense of creating new, stand-alone program sites. Policies might include direct subsidies to families for public transportation in cities with existing mass transit (e.g., designated bus passes). In the urban fringes or in rural areas, subsidies might be necessary to transport children to existing programs by providing dedicated transportation to after-school programs in nearby communities.

Whether programs need to be expanded, sustained, or created fresh, another necessary initiative will be building an appropriate pool of professionals and volunteers to work in the after-school programs. After-school programs can provide anything from simple supervision of free play to sophisticated programs of talent development, consumer and political education, and community service. Each of these kinds of programs needs staff with specific skills. Although the skill sets will vary with the type of program, public policy needs to take a close look at overall competence standards for program providers. Initiatives should also be developed that increase the pool of workers. For example, volunteers from national service programs such as AmeriCorps and Senior Corps might be specifically designated and trained to work in after-school programs. Federal and state departments of labor could also provide opportunities for training of high school youths in after-school programs, followed by their part-time employment in those same after-school programs, an initiative that would be doubly beneficial and thus highly cost effective. Youth employment programs could provide a pool of trained service providers to offer supervised, enriching activities for younger children. Working in these programs could offer high school students in the community important skills and experiences for the transition to adulthood, including an understanding of the importance of civic engagement and community service. Recall from a discussion earlier in this volume that students in upper elementary grades and beyond who engage in authentic community service benefit in many ways, including increases in positive behavior, decreases in negative behavior, improvements in academic achievement, and the development of a positive self-concept.

Another Look at Schools

I have already discussed at some length the research evidence documenting programs and practices that successfully address children's aggressive and antisocial behavior in schools. In that discussion, a number of site-specific policies, including zero tolerance discipline, anti-bullying regulations, and school bus safety regulations, were discussed in the context of program initiatives that could promote positive behavior development and engagement in school. Here I will turn to broader policies that might encourage schools to work in concert with communities and might inform teacher preparation programs.

Empowering children and youths to give back to their communities through service-learning projects is an important general policy for schools and school districts to consider for students throughout their school careers. One major element of developing a sense of responsibility and empowerment in children and adolescents is through their thoughtful engagement in meaningful community service. Service learning allows children and youths to see that they are important members of their community who serve as resources for the greater good; such an attitude is incompatible with the development of antisocial behavior. Service learning also instills in students an understanding that service to others and to the community is an important part of personal and civic life. Student achievement, student engagement and attendance, and student conduct all benefit from the establishment of service-learning programs (Walker, 1999). Although most of the evidence comes from studies of high school students, there is growing evidence that service-learning projects can benefit students both morally and intellectually at younger ages as

well (Goldsmith, Arbreton & Bradshaw, 2004). This evidence suggests that developmentally appropriate service-learning opportunities involving substantive tasks give students as young as nine the
skills and positive motivation to fully participate in the life of their
own community and understand the importance of membership in a
civil society. School districts across the country should therefore
seriously consider a policy of service learning for all students.

Examples abound of valuable and developmentally appropriate
service-learning opportunities that are directly tied to academic
skills. I am personally familiar with a project conducted by an after-
school program for elementary school students who lived in public
housing and wanted to make a difference in their immediate community. The residential neighborhood included a large open space with a
mix of concrete, grass, and sand that was equipped with swings, a
slide, and a climbing tower. However, neither the grounds nor the
equipment was in good repair, and young adults often loitered in the
area. Parents were not willing to allow their elementary-school-age
children to use the area because of the potential danger from the
aging and dirty equipment, the unkempt grounds filled with glass
and debris, and the perceived danger from other residents. The
students in grades 3–6, by their own account, were aware that they
had lost access to their playground, and they wanted it back. The
after-school provider, in partnership with the housing community's
resident advisory council, agreed to supervise the playground if
funds could be found to rehabilitate the space. After unsuccessful
attempts to secure grant funds, the students in the after-school program took on the project. With assistance from the residents and the
after-school program staff, a group of fifteen students aged eight to
twelve developed and drew quite detailed plans, drawn to scale, of a
new playground. They also searched the Internet for images and
vendors of appropriate playground equipment, ultimately compiling
a comprehensive presentation of their vision for the playground

space. The after-school staff invited the media to observe what the children had accomplished so far, and with media attention came an invitation from the city councilperson's office to make a presentation to the public housing authority. Parents, other residents, and not a few of the after-school service providers attended the students' presentation at the city hall, and their presentation, conducted without the help of adult voices, carried the day. In roughly twelve months, these students identified a problem and developed a solution that commanded a fair and respectful hearing from city leaders. As a result, municipal funds were found to build and maintain the new playground. In less than twenty-four months, these students had seen the progression from a needs assessment, to the formulation of a plan, to engagement with the political structure, to a solution to their identified need. Although this project was not accomplished as a formal service-learning activity with the local school, it demonstrates the potential of such a policy for students in any grade.

The benefit of service learning, as evidenced by this project, is the development and application of particular intellectual skills to perform needed services that produce tangible results for all of the children in the community. The students who developed their playground made remarkable gains in their math ability, from skills as simple as reading a ruler to the geometry skills needed to construct a scale drawing. However, the impact of this project on the local school and community was limited to the children in this one program who had an interest in this particular playground. A district-wide policy of engaging students with their local community could have much broader benefits for students, schools, and communities.

Implementing such a policy at the school-district level requires that schools and communities think carefully about the challenges that might occur in building a collaborative relationship between the school and the surrounding community. As the most visible formal institution in many communities and the one shared by a majority of resident families, schools can serve as a focal point for the development of healthy communities that nurture competent and responsible children. However, the complex process of bringing schools and communities together requires a collaborative relationship in which the voices of all stakeholders, including community businesses and organizations, school staff, parents, and children, are shared and valued. Thus, leadership must typically come from the highest levels of school districts and communities. To implement such a policy effectively, school superintendents and principals must publicly support such activities as a value. Community members must, in turn, demonstrate their support by providing their time and resources. Such support can come in the form of providing equipment and material for projects that students develop (as was the case for the playground project). Alternatively, business and civic leaders in the community can provide leadership, resources, and training opportunities for student service-learning projects such as community beautification (e.g., tree planting), health promotion (e.g., volunteer service at community health fairs), and school improvement (e.g., library book drive, school drama productions for the community). The point is that an effective service-learning policy must be implemented with careful, planned collaboration structures that bring together the school and the community to link appropriate projects with the school curriculum.

Because no policy change exists in a vacuum, a broadly implemented policy of service learning would call for complementary changes in the school context. Perhaps foremost among the changes at school would be that teachers and administrators would be explicitly prepared to work collaboratively with families and communities. Such a change could benefit not only the implementation of service learning but also more generally the reduction of children's aggression, because, as we have seen, the home and the school are two primary settings for the development of childhood aggression

(Laub & Lauritsen, 1998). Educators must see themselves, not just as classroom or building leaders, but as active and equal partners in the communities that host their schools and nurture their students. Each of these partners must collaborate successfully to link authentic service-learning experiences to student learning in classrooms and to maintain important ties with families to forestall aggressive behavior. A collaborative posture tends to facilitate links between home, school, and community.

I choose the term *collaborate* intentionally. A true collaborative relationship is one in which each partner receives help in achieving objectives while helping other partners achieve their objectives (Corrigan, 2000). For each partner, collaboration requires a certain amount of letting go of power, privilege, and business as usual; rather, each works so that all may succeed. Essentially, each member of any collaboration becomes an agent for the other members. Such respect, trust, and confidence in others takes time to build and cannot be imposed by any one member; schools in particular would be unwise to stake sole claim to "expert" knowledge of what communities and families need to do. Each partner will need to adopt a posture of respectful listening and collaboration. Professional educators are often explicitly trained in professional collaboration among teachers, administrators, and designated service providers (e.g., psychologists, speech specialists). But the training in collaboration beyond the bounds of education professionals is often limited or nonexistent.

Thus, training for both teachers and administrators (pre-service and in-service) must explicitly attend to skills necessary for collaboration with families and communities. University teacher-preparation programs and district in-service training must explicitly provide content and strategies that teach educators to build partnerships. Research in teacher education shows that developing these skills for partnership improves teaches' beliefs that they can successfully collaborate with families and communities, and these positive beliefs lead to increased use of the skills (Garcia, 2004). Programs should enable teachers to become competent in collaborations that integrate the goals and work of parents, schools, and community members (youth services, businesses, health services, etc.). For example, teachers need skills to work with other adults, not just with children. Building partnerships requires adult-to-adult communication skills with a broad range of people beyond the community of education professionals. Every school professional also needs some training in group dynamics and group processes. School professionals need to know how and when to facilitate groups, lead groups, and support group leaders. Cooperative learning as a pedagogical strategy is an important part of current teacher-preparation curricula; working successfully in groups with other adult equals should be a similarly important part of the curriculum for prospective and practicing teachers.

Experience in working with adult groups as well as with families is best gained through direct contact with families and communities (Shartrand, Kreider & Erickson-Warfield, 1994). Therefore, teacher preparation programs should seriously consider the value of experiential and service-learning programs for their students. For example, students might survey the school, family, and community connections that exist at their student-teaching sites and develop a tangible plan to initiate a relationship that responds to an identified need in the community (Grinberg & Goldfarb, 1998). The plan might then be provided to the supervising teacher and building administrator for possible implementation. For example, a plan to mobilize families, community, and school to advocate together before local and state governments for funds to develop an after-school program could benefit children's behavior and achievement, family-school relations, and the quality of community efficacy.

Arguably the most significant policy for pre-service and in-service teacher education is the development and dissemination of materials to develop cultural competence among education professionals. Fortunately, it is probably no longer necessary to ask why cultural competence is such a central skill for education professionals and has such influence on efforts to prevent aggression and violence. There is compelling evidence that practices, educational or otherwise, developed for one cultural context may not apply successfully in another. These findings are unsurprising once we realize that culture is the system that organizes a group's adaptation to a unique environment. This systems view (Kitayama, 2002) sees culture as a set of meanings (e.g., beliefs, values, goals) that are shared by an identifiable group of people and shape their ways of living (Betancourt & López, 1993). These sets of meanings organize group members' associated behaviors (e.g., social norms, communication styles, rituals) so members will succeed in the cultural and ecological contexts that frame their daily lives. Culture is the medium in which we develop and enact our relations with and expectations for others. Thus, in the multicultural society of the United States, each of us must learn to successfully interact with those whose culture differs, substantially or subtly, from our own. It is important to remember that ethnic match is no guarantee of cultural compatibility among participants in any endeavor.

In a model of cultural competence that I have presented elsewhere (Hudley & Taylor, 2006), I define in three subdomains of efficacy in multicultural environments. The subdomain of cultural competence relevant to the discussion of teacher education policy is labeled *culturally effective*. This subdomain refers to the requisite self-knowledge, attitudes, and skills that allow education professionals to work and collaborate successfully with people from a broad range of cultural backgrounds.

Self-knowledge, the first criterion for culturally effective functioning, represents both an awareness of one's own cultural worldview and the understanding that everyone's worldview is the product of prior life history and experience. In the diverse U.S. society we find multiple worldviews constructed by a range of factors that include social class, ethnicity, language, gender, and institutional power relations. Self-knowledge can lead to an understanding of how other participants' cultural systems organize beliefs and behavior because it makes visible the ability of our own worldview to distort our understanding of others. Someone who is culturally effective possesses an attitude of appreciation for the culture of each member in a collaborative group. Each person's culture can be understood as a system of living, thinking, talking, and so forth, that represents an adaptation to the particular demands of his or her dynamic ecocultural niche. The culture of the dominant group (i.e., middle-class Whites) is understood to enjoy high status owing to institutionalized power inequality rather than inherent superiority. Culturally effective skills may be specific to particular groups or may be attributed to a more general competence in working in multicultural settings. Skills specific to a particular group are the product of explicit knowledge of that group, including the economic, social, and political pressures present in the group's unique ecocultural niche. For example, a culturally effective teacher takes time to know and understand students and their families and communities. Culturally effective educators are also committed to a safe and just future for all children, which makes social justice is a high priority. Although some combination of skills and attitudes for working in culturally diverse classrooms and schools may be a part of some university programs of teacher education, neither explicit attention to cultural competence for prospective teachers and administrators nor uniform standards for assessing such competence is mandated policy for all programs. This is an urgent national priority.

Cultural competence is a developmental process that needs to be revisited periodically. Culture is a complex, evolving, living system that cannot be reified in a teacher preparation curriculum or training manual. Thus, the education profession should seriously consider a policy of ongoing in-service education and training, similar to the continuing education expected for counseling and medical professionals. A central feature of continuing education should be program- and self-evaluation to assure that school programs and community collaboration efforts are relevant to the partners and to students with whom they work.

The Family-Friendly Workplace

After-school care and active school-community collaborations are critical because many, if not most, families have primary caregivers of school-age children in the workplace full-time. Roughly three out of four mothers of school-age children are in the workforce, most of them full-time, and the proportion is substantially higher in low-income households. Interestingly, the single-parent family with an employed father at its head is the fastest growing category of family in the country, according to the Bureau of Labor Statistics. Thus, single-parent households in various forms are the reality of family life into the foreseeable future.

The need to combine full-time work and successful child-rearing has been the impetus for an important public conversation focused on family-friendly policies in the workplace, a debate that has obvious connections to concerns about children's after-school lives and parental supervision. Family-friendly policies help employees succeed both in a given workplace and at home. Workplace policies that allow parents to monitor and care for children while they remain successful employees can protect against not only the development of antisocial behavior in children but also stress, depression, and other mental health problems in overextended working parents. A parent working full-time, depending on the nature and demands of the job, may have less time to spend with children of all ages than a parent who is not employed or is employed part-time (Nomaguchi, Milkie & Bianchi, 2005). A *single* working parent spends the least amount of time of any parent on personal or leisure activities. Relaxed, leisurely time spent listening to, sharing with, and enjoying children and family builds the positive, nurturing climate that is so important for raising children who are emotionally healthy and not prone to aggressive or antisocial behavior. Children can see that their parents make time for them and their lives and may disclose information about their lives when parents are seen as warm and accepting.

A work environment that provides the support for parents to spend time with children is good not only for children but also for parental mental and emotional health (Hill, 2005). Parents who spend time with their children can feel positive about their level of concern and commitment to them. Working parents (Weigel et al., 1995), mothers in particular (Hays, 1996), often report that they feel resentful of a partner if they are married, isolated and overwhelmed if they are single, and that they lack a reliable network of social support (Hill, 2005; Shipley & Coats, 1992). Parental employment in general is certainly not a direct predictor of negative outcomes in children's behavior, does not automatically decrease the time available for children (Bianchi, 2000), and can have many positive benefits for low-income children (Secret & Peck-Heath, 2004). Rather, lack of time for self and family is a major cause of parental stress and burnout at work and at home (Nomaguchi, Milkie & Bianchi, 2005) in the same way that lack of time to monitor children is an important contributor to children's aggressive antisocial behavior. A workplace that is organized to facilitate parental time for family responsibilities while maintaining high levels of productivity and job satisfaction is good for children, good for parents, and good for employers.

A number of workplace policies and services are able to support parents in their efforts to monitor and nurture their children and thereby avert the development of aggressive and antisocial behavior. Perhaps the most frequently cited policies that can give working parents some time for family are job sharing, flexible hours, and telecommuting. Job sharing can often give parents access to more interesting and satisfying jobs than are often available in the traditional part-time employment sector (retail, food service, service) without the level of time investment that might be needed for a full-time position. Flexible hours allow parents to tailor their work life to fit their family's needs. Telecommuting similarly allows parents to be more present in the home and in their children's lives. Attending a child's performance, going along on a field trip, volunteering in the classroom, and walking a child to school are just a few of the activities that might be more available to parents whose employers have policies that provide some personal control over their time. Sharing such activities allows parents to learn about their children's lives and friends, allows children an opportunity for positive parental attention, and allows parents and children to strengthen their bonds of mutual trust and affection. As employees gain control over their time, they can balance work and family responsibilities, become involved in activities that are important to their children, and take advantage of opportunities to monitor, nurture, and listen to their children. This represents the kind of parental caring that decreases the risk of childhood aggression.

Family-friendly work policies also include decisions by employers to devote resources to direct services to parents. For example, parents often need help with the many tasks that come with raising children and adolescents. Identifying quality child care, educational services, community enrichment programs, and other opportunities can be time consuming and even bewildering for some parents. However, companies can put resources into hiring paid staff or consultants to help parents navigate their communities' services and maximize their children's positive development. Companies might also provide a time and place for parents to meet together as a support group in which members can share parenting and/or child care resource and referral information. Again, paid professionals who provide parenting training and counseling might also be an invaluable addition to such parent groups. Simple opportunities to share experiences and get feedback can be an excellent source of support for parents going through the difficult times that come with the role of parent.

Companies can put resources toward a variety of other services as well, large and small, that benefit children both directly and indirectly. Child care services and subsidies are becoming a standard part of corporate culture. Although most companies' policies presume a need for full-day services for children at toddler and preschool ages, awareness is dawning of the need for care at all of a child's stages of development (Vandell, Pierce & Dadisman, 2005). During middle childhood, family-friendly policies might include support for after-school services, sick child care, and mentoring programs. Even a policy as simple as making a telephone accessible to employees who work in places other than office settings can allow parents, particularly low-wage workers who may not own a cell phone, to remain in touch with children. Each kind of program has its own influence on children's development and behavior by providing monitoring, nurturing, and positive attention for children who might otherwise be unsupervised.

Finally, the need for a more effective health-care policy in this country is beyond question. Germane to this discussion is the need for mental health services for parents and children. To repeat the earlier point from our scenario of the harried family, the mental and emotional strains of balancing the demands of home and work as a part of daily life can create inconsistent and harsh parenting and even child abuse, any of which bring substantial consequences for children's aggressive behaviors. Providing counseling for parents, children, spouses, and families as needed, whether on-site or as part of a health-benefits package, may be one of the most powerful and effective family-friendly services that an employer can provide for parents.

This admittedly selective discussion of policy is intended to describe a few of the things that we as individuals, members of families, supporters of schools, residents of communities, and contributors to society might do to support positive behaviors in all children. Child-focused interventions such as the Brainpower Program, albeit important in their own right, can make scant headway against children's aggression if used alone. In previous chapters I described the evidence for engaging the several systems that have impact on the child (family, school, peers) and some of the specific interventions that can be used in tandem with BrainPower. In this final chapter we can see how such efforts might be supported, at the broadest levels of our society, by communities, corporations, and government. Only a concerted effort by all stakeholders working together will ensure that our children and youths successfully navigate positive trajectories toward adulthood.

References

Albee, G. 1982. Preventing psychopathology and promoting human potential. *American Psychologist, 37,* 1043–1050.

Allard, P., and Young, M. 2002. Prosecuting juveniles in adult court: Perspectives for policymakers and practitioners. The Sentencing Project. Online. Available at http://www.sentencingproject.org/pdfs/2079.pdf.

Arnold, D. 1997. Co-occurrence of externalizing behavior problems and emergent academic difficulties in young high-risk boys: A preliminary evaluation of patterns and mechanisms. *Journal of Applied Developmental Psychology, 18,* 317–330.

Arnold, D., Homrok, S., Ortiz, C., and Stowe, R. 1999. Direct observation of peer rejection acts and their temporal relation with aggressive acts. *Early Childhood Research Quarterly, 14,* 183–196.

Associated Press. 2007. 3 Long Island teens arrested in girl's beating shown online. *The Associated Press State and Local Wire* (January 17). Retrieved February 20, 2007, from http://web.lexis-nexis.com/universe/document?—m=f08935df3d6206eec39681.

Astor, R., Meyer, H., Benbenishty, R., Marachi, R., and Rosemond, M. 2005. School safety interventions: Best practices and programs. *Children and Schools, 27,* 17–32.

Barnow, S., Lucht, M., and Freyberger, H. 2005. Correlates of aggressive and delinquent conduct problems in adolescence. *Aggressive Behavior, 31,* 24–39.

Baumrind, D. 1978. Parental disciplinary patterns and social competence in children. *Youth and Society, 9,* 239–276.

Belle, D., and Doucet, J. 2003. Poverty, inequality, and discrimination as sources of depression among U.S. women. *Psychology of Women Quarterly*, 27, 101–113.

Benson, P. 1990. *The troubled journey: A portrait of 6th–12th-grade youth.* Minneapolis, MN: Search Institute.

———. 1997. *All kids are our kids: What communities must do to raise caring and responsible children and adolescents.* San Francisco: Jossey-Bass.

Betancourt, H., and López, S. 1993. The study of culture, ethnicity, and race in American psychology. *American Psychologist, 48,* 629–637.

Bianchi, S. 2000. Maternal employment and time with children: Dramatic change or surprising continuity? *Demography, 37,* 401–414.

Bierman, K. 2004. *Peer rejection: Developmental processes and intervention strategies.* New York: Guilford.

Bierman, K., Bruschi, C., Domitorvich, C., Fang, G., Miller-Johnson, S., and Conduct Problems Prevention Research Group. 2004. Early disruptive behaviors associated with emerging antisocial behavior among girls. In M. Putallaz and K. Bierman, eds., *Aggression, antisocial behavior, and violence among girls: A developmental perspective* (pp. 137–161). New York: Guilford.

Binns, K., and Markow, D. 1999. *The Metropolitan Life survey of the American teacher, 1999: Violence in America's public schools—five years later.* New York: Metropolitan Life Insurance Co.

Blechman, E., and Vryan, K. 2000. Prosocial family therapy: A manualized preventive intervention for juvenile offenders. *Aggression and Violent Behavior, 5,* 343–378.

Bohannon, H. 2006. Schoolwide application of positive behavior support in an urban high school: A case study. *Journal of Positive Behavioral Interventions, 8,* 131–145.

Bould, S. 2003. Caring neighborhoods: Bringing up the kids together. *Journal of Family Issues, 24,* 427–447.

Bowen, G., and Chapman, M. 1996. Poverty, neighborhood danger, social support, and the individual adaptation among at-risk youth in urban areas. *Journal of Family Issues, 17,* 641–666.

Bowlby, J. 1980. *Attachment and loss.* New York: Basic Books.

Broidy, L., Nagin, D., Tremblay, R., Bates, J., Brame, B., Dodge, K., Fergusson, D., Horwood, J., Loeber, R., Laird, R., Lynam, D., Moffitt,

T., Pettit, G., and Vitaro, F. 2003. Developmental trajectories of child-hood disruptive behaviors and adolescent delinquency: A six-site cross-national study. *Developmental Psychology, 39,* 222–245.

Brookmeyer, K., Henrich, C., and Schwab-Stone, M. 2005. Adolescents who witness community violence: Can parent support and prosocial cognitions protect them from committing violence? *Child Development, 76,* 917–929.

Bugental, D., and Grusec, J. 2006. Socialization processes. In N. Eisen-berg, W. Damon, and R. Lerner, eds., *Handbook of child psychology,* vol. 3: *Social, emotional, and personality development,* 6th ed. (pp. 366–428). Hoboken, NJ: Wiley.

Burgess, K., Wojslawowicz, J., Rubin, K., Rose-Krasnor, L., and Booth-LaForce, C. 2006. Social information processing and coping strat-egies of shy/withdrawn and aggressive children: Does friendship matter? *Child Development, 77,* 371–383.

Cairns, R., and Cairns, B. 1994. *Lifelines and risks: Pathways of youth in our time.* Cambridge: Cambridge University Press.

Cairns, R., Cairns, B., and Neckerman, H. 1989. Early school dropout: Configurations and determinants. *Child Development, 60,* 1437–1452.

Cairns, R., Cairns, B., Neckerman, H., Ferguson, L., and Gariépy, J. 1989. Growth and aggression: I. Childhood to early adolescence. *De-velopmental Psychology, 25,* 320–330.

Cairns, R., Cairns, B., Neckerman, H., Gest, S., and Gariépy, J. 1988. Social networks and aggressive behavior: Peer support or peer rejec-tion? *Developmental Psychology, 24,* 815–823.

Casella, R. 2000. The benefits of peer mediation in the context of urban conflict and program status. *Urban Education, 35,* 324–355.

Cavell, T. 2000. *Working with parents of aggressive children: A practi-tioner's guide.* Washington, DC: American Psychological Association.

Chen, X., Rubin, K., and Li, D. 1997. Relation between academic achievement and social adjustment: Evidence from Chinese children. *Developmental Psychology, 33,* 518–525.

Christenson, S., Hirsch, J., and Hurley, C. 1997. Families with aggressive children and adolescents. In A. Goldstein and J. Conoley, eds., *School violence intervention: A practical handbook* (pp. 325–365). New York: Guilford.

Coie, J., and Dodge, K. 1988. Multiple sources of data on social behavior and social status in the school: A cross-age comparison. *Child Development*, 59, 815–829.

Coie, J., and Kupersmidt, J. 1983. A behavioral analysis of emerging social status in boys' groups. *Child Development*, 54, 1400–1416.

Coie, J., Terry, R., Lenox, K., Lochman, J., and Hyman, C. 1995. Childhood peer rejection and aggression as predictors of stable patterns of adolescent disorder. *Development and Psychopathology*, 7, 697–713.

Coleman, S. 2006. Antibullying effort has a local push. *Boston Globe* (October 22).

Conduct Problems Prevention Research Group. 2002. The implementation of the Fast Track Program: An example of a large-scale prevention science efficacy trial. *Journal of Abnormal Child Psychology*, 30, 19–35.

Connor, D. 2002. *Aggression and antisocial behavior in children and adolescents: Research and treatment*. New York: Guilford.

Corrigan, D. 2000. The changing role of schools and higher education institutions with respect to community-based interagency collaboration and interprofessional partnerships. *Peabody Journal of Education*, 75, 176–195.

Crick, N. 1997. Engagement in gender normative versus nonnormative forms of aggression: Links to social-psychological adjustment. *Developmental Psychology*, 33, 610–617.

Crick, N., and Rose, A. 2000. Toward a gender-balanced approach to the study of social-emotional development: A look at relational aggression. In P. Miller and E. Kofsky Scholnick, eds., *Toward a feminist developmental psychology* (pp. 153–168). Florence, KY: Taylor and Frances / Routledge.

Crittenden, P., and Ainsworth, M. 1989. Child maltreatment and attachment theory. In D. Cicchetti and V. Carlson, eds., *Child maltreatment: Theory and research on the causes and consequences of child abuse and neglect* (pp. 432–463). New York: Cambridge University Press.

Deater-Deckard, K., and Dodge, K. 1997. Externalizing behavior problems and discipline revisited: Nonlinear effects and variation by culture, context, and gender. *Psychological Inquiry*, 8, 161–175.

Dishion, T., and Dodge K. 2005. Peer contagion in interventions for children and adolescents: Moving towards an understanding of the ecology and dynamics of change. *Journal of Abnormal Child Psychology, 33,* 395–400.

Dishion, T. J., Spracklen, K. M., Andrews, D. W., and Patterson, G. R. 1996. Deviancy training in male adolescent friendships. *Behavior Therapy, 27,* 373–390.

Dodge, K. 1980. Social cognition and children's aggressive behavior. *Child Development, 51,* 162–170.

Dodge, K., Coie, J., and Lynam, D. 2006. Aggression and antisocial behavior in youth. In N. Eisenberg, W. Damon, and R. Lerner, eds., *Handbook of child psychology,* vol. 3: *Social, emotional, and personality development,* 6th ed. (pp. 719–788). Hoboken, NJ: Wiley.

Dodge, K., Dishion, T., and Lansford, J. 2006. *Deviant peer influences in programs for youth: Problems and solutions.* New York: Guilford.

Dodge, K., and Frame, C. 1982. Social cognitive biases and deficits in aggressive boys. *Child Development, 53,* 620–635.

Dodge, K., Lansford, J., Burks, V., Bates, J., Pettit, G., Fontaine, R., and Price, J. 2003. Peer rejection and social information-processing factors in the development of aggressive behavior problems in children. *Child Development, 74,* 374–393.

Dodge, K., Murphy, R., and Buchsbaum, K. 1984. The assessment of intention cue detection skills in children. *Child Development, 55,* 163–173.

Dodge, K., and Newman, J. 1981. Biased decision-making processes in aggressive boys. *Journal of Abnormal Psychology, 90,* 375–379.

Dodge, K., Petit, G., and Bates, J. 1997. How the experience of early physical abuse leads children to become chronically aggressive. In D. Cicchetti and S. Toth, eds., *Developmental perspectives on trauma: Theory, research, and intervention* (pp. 263–288). Rochester Symposium on Developmental Psychopathology, vol. 8. Rochester, NY: University of Rochester Press.

Dodge, K., and Tomlin, A. 1987. Utilization of self-schema as a mechanism of interpersonal bias in aggressive children. *Social Cognition, 5,* 280–300.

Downey, G., Lebolt, A., Rincón, C., and Freitas, A. 1998. Rejection sensitivity and children's interpersonal difficulties. *Child Development, 69,* 1074–1091.

Dubow, E., Huesmann, L. R., Boxer, P., Pulkkinen, L., and Kokko, K. 2006. Middle childhood and adolescent contextual and personal predictors of adult educational and occupational outcomes: A mediational model in two countries. *Developmental Psychology, 42,* 937–949.

Eamon, M., and Venkataraman, M. 2003. Implementing parent management training in the context of poverty. *American Journal of Family Therapy, 31,* 281–293.

Ehrensaft, M., Cohen, P., Brown, J., Smailes, E., Chen, H., and Johnson, J. 2003. Intergenerational transmission of partner violence: A 20-year prospective study. *Journal of Consulting and Clinical Psychology, 71,* 741–753.

Ensminger, M., and Slusarcick, A. 1992. Paths to high school graduation or drop out: A longitudinal study of a first grade cohort. *Sociology of Education, 65,* 95–113.

Eronen, S., and Nurmi, J. 2001. Sociometric status of young adults: Behavioural correlates, and cognitive-motivational antecedents and consequences. *International Journal of Behavioral Development, 25,* 203–213.

Farrell, A., and Bruce, S. 1997. Impact of exposure to community violence on violent behavior and emotional distress among urban adolescents. *Journal of Clinical Child Psychology, 26,* 2–14.

Farrington, D. 1994. Childhood, adolescent, and adult features of violent males. In L. R. Huesmann, ed., *Aggressive behavior: Current perspectives* (pp. 215–240). New York: Plenum.

Finzi, R., Ram, A., Har-Even, D., Shnit, D., and Weizman, A. 2001. Attachment styles and aggression in physically abused and neglected children. *Journal of Youth and Adolescence, 30,* 769–786.

Forsterling, F. 1985. Attribution retraining: A review. *Psychological Bulletin, 98,* 495–512.

Fredricks, J., and Eccles, J. 2006. Extracurricular involvement and adolescent adjustment: Impact of duration, number of activities, and breadth of participation. *Applied Developmental Science, 10,* 132–146.

French, D., and Conrad, J. 2001. School dropout as predicted by peer rejection and antisocial behavior. *Journal of Research on Adolescence,* *11*, 225–244.

Garcia, D. 2004. Exploring connections between the construct of teacher efficacy and family involvement practices: Implications for urban teacher preparation. *Urban Education, 39*, 290–315.

Garner, R., Zhao, Y., and Gillingham, M. 2002. *Hanging out: Community-based after-school program for children.* Westport, CT: Bergin and Garvey.

Gifford-Smith, M., and Rabiner, D. 2004. The relation between social information processing and children's social adjustment: An updated review of the literature. In J. Kupersmidt and K. Dodge, eds., *Children's peer relations: From development to intervention.* Washington, DC, American Psychological Association.

Gillies, R., and Ashman, A. 2003. *Co-operative learning: The social and intellectual outcomes of learning in groups.* New York: Routledge.

Goldsmith, J., Arbreton, A., and Bradshaw, M. 2004. *Promoting emotional and behavioral health in preteens: Benchmarks of success and challenges among programs in Santa Clara and San Mateo counties.* Palo Alto, CA: Lucille Packard Foundation.

Goldstein, A. 1994. *The ecology of aggression.* New York: Plenum.

Graham, S., and Hudley, C. 1994. Attributions of aggressive and nonaggressive African-American male early adolescents: A study of construct accessibility. *Developmental Psychology, 30*, 365–373.

Graham, S., Hudley, C., and Williams, E. 1992. Attributional and emotional determinants of aggression among African-American and Latino young adolescents. *Developmental Psychology, 28*, 731–740.

Graham, S., Taylor, A., and Hudley, C. 1998. Exploring achievement values among ethnic minority early adolescents. *Journal of Educational Psychology, 90*, 606–620.

Granger, R. 2002. Creating the conditions linked to positive youth development. *New Directions for Youth Development, 95*, 149–164.

Green, B., Bailey, J., and Barber, F. 1981. An analysis and reduction of disruptive behavior on school buses. *Journal of Applied Behavior Analysis, 14*, 177–192.

Gresham, F., and Elliot, S. 1990. *The Social Skills Rating System.* Circle Pines, MN: American Guidance Service.

Grinberg, J., and Goldfarb, K. 1998. Moving teacher education in/to the community. *Theory into Practice, 37*, 131–139.

Haapasalo, J., and Tremblay, R. 1994. Physically aggressive boys from ages 6 to 12: Family background, parenting behavior, and prediction of delinquency. *Journal of Consulting and Clinical Psychology, 62*, 1044–1052.

Harvey, J., and Galvin, K. 1984. Clinical implications of attribution theory and research. *Clinical Psychology Review, 4*, 15–33.

Haselager, G., Cillessen, A., Van Lieshout, C., Riksen-Walraven, J., and Hartup, W. 2002. Heterogeneity among peer-rejected boys across middle childhood: Developmental pathways of social behavior. *Developmental Psychology, 38*, 446–456.

Hays, S. 1996. *The cultural contradictions of motherhood.* New Haven: Yale University Press.

Hill, E. J. 2005. Work-family facilitation and conflict, working fathers and mothers, work-family stressors and support. *Journal of Family Issues, 26*, 793–819.

Hinshaw, S. 1992. Externalizing behavior problems and academic underachievement in childhood and adolescence: Causal relationships and underlying mechanisms. *Psychological Bulletin, 111*, 127–155.

Hoffman, M. 2000. *Empathy and moral development: Implications for caring and justice.* New York: Cambridge University Press.

Horn, J., and Trickett, P. 1998. Community violence and child development: A review of research. In P. Trickett and C. Schellebach, eds., *Violence against children in the family and the community* (pp. 103–138). Washington, DC: American Psychological Association.

Hudley, C. 1994. The reduction of childhood aggression using the BrainPower Program. In M. Furlong and D. Smith, eds., *Anger, hostility and aggression: Assessment, prevention, and intervention strategies for youth* (pp. 313–344). Brandon, VT: Clinical Psychology Publishing Co.

———. 1995. Assessing the impact of separate schooling for African-American male adolescents. *Journal of Early Adolescence, 15*, 38–57.

———. 1997a. Supporting achievement beliefs among ethnic minority adolescents: Two case examples. *Journal of Research on Adolescence, 7*, 133–152.

———. 1997b. Teacher practices and student motivation in a middle school program for African American males. *Urban Education, 32,* 304–319.

———. 1999. Problem behaviors in middle childhood: Understanding risk status and protective factors. Paper presented at the American Educational Research Association annual meeting, Montreal, Canada, April.

———. 2001. Supporting perceptions of social and academic competence in middle childhood: Influences of a community-based youth development program. Paper presented at the American Educational Research Association annual meeting, Seattle, WA, April.

———. 2003. Cognitive-behavioral intervention with aggressive children. In M. Matson, ed., *Neurobiology of aggression: Understanding and preventing violence* (pp. 275–288). Totowa, NJ: Humana Press.

Hudley, C., Britsch, B., Wakefield, W., Smith, T., DeMorat, M., and Cho, S. 1998. An attribution retraining program to reduce aggression in elementary school students. *Psychology in the Schools, 35,* 271–282.

Hudley, C., and Friday, J. 1996 Attributional bias and reactive aggression. *American Journal of Preventive Medicine, 12* (suppl. 1), 75–81.

Hudley, C., and Graham, S. 1993. An attributional intervention to reduce peer directed aggression among African-American boys. *Child Development, 64,* 124–138.

———. 1994. Attributions for social outcomes: A comparison of mothers of aggressive and nonaggressive sons. Poster presented at the biennial meeting of the Society for Research on Adolescence, San Diego, CA.

Hudley, C., & Novak, A. 2007. Environmental influences, the developing brain, and aggressive behavior. *Theory into Practice, 46,* 121–129.

Hudley, C., and Taylor, A. 2006. Cultural competence and youth violence prevention programming. In N. Guerra and E. Smith, eds., *Ethnicity, culture, and youth violence prevention programming* (pp. 249–269). Washington DC: American Psychological Association.

Huesmann, L. R. 1998. The role of social information processing and cognitive schema in the acquisition and maintenance of habitual aggressive behavior. In R. Geen and E. Donnerstein, eds., *Human aggression: Theories, research, and implications for social policy* (pp. 73–109). San Diego: Academic Press.

Huesmann, L. R., Dubow, E., Eron, L., and Boxer, P. 2006. Middle childhood family-contextual and personal factors as predictors of adult outcomes. In A. Huston and M. Ripke, eds., *Developmental contexts in middle childhood: Bridges to adolescence and adulthood* (pp. 62–86). New York: Cambridge University Press.

Huesmann, L. R., Eron, L., Lefkowitz, M., and Walder, L. 1984. Stability of aggression over time and generations. *Developmental Psychology, 20*, 1120–1134.

Huesmann, L. R., and Reynolds, M. 2001. Cognitive processes and the development of aggression. In A. Bohart and D. Stipek. eds., *Constructive and destructive behavior: Implications for family, school, and society* (pp. 249–269). Washington, DC: American Psychological Association.

Huston, A., and Ripke, M. 2006. *Developmental contexts in middle childhood: Bridges to adolescence and adulthood.* New York: Cambridge University Press.

Hymel, S., Wagner, E., and Butler, L. 1990. Reputational bias: View from the peer group. In S. Asher and J. Coie. eds., *Peer rejection in childhood* (pp. 156–186). New York: Cambridge University Press.

Ialongo, N., Vaden-Kiernan, N., and Kellam, S. 1998. Early peer rejection and aggression: Longitudinal relations with adolescent behavior. *Journal of Developmental and Physical Disabilities, 10*, 199–213.

Ingoldsby, E., and Shaw, D. 2002. Neighborhood contextual factors and early-starting antisocial pathways. *Clinical Child and Family Psychology Review, 5*, 21–55.

Institute of Medicine. 1994. *Reducing risks for mental disorders: Frontiers for preventive intervention research.* Washington, DC: National Academy Press.

Jacobsen, N., and Truax, P. 1991. Clinical significance: A statistical approach to defining meaningful change in psychotherapy research. *Journal of Consulting and Clinical Psychology, 59*, 12–19.

Jarrett, R., and Jefferson, S. 2004. Women's danger management strategies in an inner-city housing project. *Family Relations, 53*, 138–147.

Johnson, D., and Johnson, R. 1995. Teaching students to be peace makers: Results of five years of research. *Peace and Conflict: Journal of Peace Psychology, 1*, 417–438.

——. 1996. Conflict resolution and peer mediation programs in elementary and secondary schools: A review of the research. *Review of Educational Research, 66,* 459–506.

——. 2004. Implementing the "Teaching Students to Be *Peacemakers*" program. *Theory into Practice, 43,* 68–79.

Kasen, S., Johnson, J., and Cohen, P. 1990. The impact of school emotional climate on student psychopathology. *Journal of Abnormal Child Psychology, 18,* 165–177.

Kazdin, A. 1980. *Research design in clinical psychology.* New York: Harper and Row.

Kazdin, A. 2005. *Parent management training: Treatment for oppositional, aggressive, and antisocial behavior in children and adolescents.* New York: Oxford University Press.

Kelley, H. 1973. The process of causal attribution. *American Psychologist, 28,* 107–128.

Kempf-Leonard, K., Chesney-Lind, M., and Hawkins, D. 2001. In R. Lober and D. Farrington. eds., *Child delinquents: Development, intervention, and service needs* (pp. 247–269). Thousand Oaks, CA: Sage.

Kemple, J., and Snipes, J. 2000. *Career academies: Impacts on students' engagement and performance in high school.* New York: MDRC.

Kitayama, S. 2002. Culture and basic psychological processes—Toward a system view of culture: Comment on Oyserman et al. 2002. *Psychological Bulletin, 128,* 89–96.

Kitsantas, A., Ware, H., and Martinez-Arias, R. 2004. Students' perceptions of school safety: Effects by community, school environment, and substance use variables. *Journal of Early Adolescence, 24,* 412–430.

Knutson, J. F., DeGarmo, D., Koeppl, G., and Reid, J. B. 2005. Care neglect, supervisory neglect, and harsh parenting in the development of children's aggression: A replication and extension. *Child maltreatment, 10,* 92–107.

Knutson, J. F., DeGarmo, D. S., and Reid, J. B. 2004. Social disadvantage and neglectful parenting as precursors to the development of antisocial and aggressive child behavior: Testing a theoretical model. *Aggressive Behavior, 30,* 187–205.

Krohn, M., Thornberry, T., Rivera, C., and Le Blanc, M. 2001. Later delinquency careers. In R. Lober and D. Farrington, eds., *Child delinquents: Development, intervention, and service needs* (pp. 67–93). Thousand Oaks, CA: Sage.

Kupersmidt, J., and DeRosier, M. 2004. How peer problems lead to negative outcomes: An integrative mediational model. In J. Kupersmidt and K. Dodge, eds., *Children's peer relations: From development to intervention* (pp. 119–138). Washington DC: American Psychological Association.

LaFontana, K. M., and Cillessen, A. H. N. 2002. Children's perceptions of popular and unpopular peers: A multimethod assessment. *Developmental Psychology, 38,* 635–647.

Laird, R., Jordan, K., Dodge, K., Pettit, G., and Bates, J. 2001. Peer rejection in childhood, involvement with antisocial peers in early adolescence, and the development of externalizing behavior problems. *Development and Psychopathology, 13,* 337–354.

Laub, J. H., and Lauritsen, J. L. 1998. The interdependence of school violence with neighborhood and family conditions. In D. S. Elliott, B. Hamburg, and K. R. Williams, eds., *Violence in American schools: A new perspective* (pp. 127–155). New York: Cambridge University Press.

Lefkowitz, M., Eron, L., Walder, L., and Huesmann, L. 1977. *Growing up to be violent: A longitudinal study of the development of aggression.* New York: Pergamon.

Lerner, R., and Benson, P. 2003. *Developmental assets and asset-building communities: Implications for research, policy, and practice.* New York: Kluwer.

Lochman, J., and Dodge, K. 1994. Social-cognitive processes of severely violent, moderately aggressive, and nonaggressive boys. *Journal of Consulting and Clinical Psychology, 62,* 366–374.

Loeber, R., Pardini, D., Homish, D., Wei, E., Crawford, A., Farrington, D., Stouthamer-Loeber, M., Creemers, J., Koehler, S., and Rosenfeld, R. 2005. The prediction of violence and homicide in young men. *Journal of Consulting and Clinical Psychology, 73,* 1074–1088.

Loeber, R., and Stouthamer-Loeber, M. 1986. Family factors as correlates and predictors of juvenile conduct problems and delinquency. In M. Tonrey and N. Morris, eds., *Crime and justice: An annual review of research* (pp. 29–149). Chicago: University of Chicago Press.

Lynch, M. 2003. Consequences of children's exposure to community violence. *Clinical Child and Family Psychology Review, 6,* 265–274.

Magee, M. 2005. City woes touch schools; 27 campuses could lose sessions before, after classes. *San Diego Union-Tribune* (May 12).

Magid, K., and McKelvey, C. 1987. *High risk: Children without a conscience.* Golden, CO: M and M Publishing.

Manly, J. T., Kim, J. E., Rogosch, F. A., and Cicchetti, D. 2001. Dimensions of child maltreatment and children's adjustment: Contributions of developmental timing and subtype. *Development and Psychopathology, 13,* 759–782.

Mannes, M., Roehlkepartain, E., and Benson, P. 2005. Unleashing the power of community to strengthen the well-being of children, youth, and families: An asset-building approach. *Child Welfare Journal, 84,* 233–250.

Masten, A., Coatsworth, J., Neemann, J., Geest, S., Tellegen, A., and Garmezy, N. 1995. The structure and coherence of competence from childhood through adolescence. *Child Development, 66,* 1635–1659.

McCord, J. 2003. Cures that harm: Unanticipated outcomes of crime prevention programs. *Annals of the American Academy of Political and Social Science, 587,* 16–30.

McDonald, L., Billingham, S., and *Conrad,* T. 1997. Families and Schools Together (FAST): Integrating community development with clinical strategies. *Families in Society, 78,* 140–155.

McLoyd, V., and Smith, J. 2002. Physical discipline and behavior problems in African American, European American, and Hispanic children: Emotional support as a moderator. *Journal of Marriage and the Family, 64,* 40–53.

McMahon, R., and Forehand, R. 2003. *Helping the noncompliant child: Family-based treatment for oppositional behavior.* 2nd ed. New York: Guilford.

McPhee, M. 2007. BHA poised to seize crime-wracked housing project. *Boston Herald* (January 14).

Metzler, C., Biglan, A., Rusby, J., and Sprague, J. 2001. Evaluation of a comprehensive behavior management program to improve school-wide positive behavior support. *Education and Treatment of Children, 24,* 448–479.

Meyer, L., and Evans, I. 1989. *Nonaversive intervention for behavior problems: A manual for home and community.* Baltimore, MD: Brookes.

Miles, S., and Stipek, D. 2006. Contemporaneous and longitudinal associations between social behavior and literacy achievement in a sample of low-income elementary school students. *Child Development, 77,* 103–117.

Minuchin , S., and Fishman, H. 1981. *Family therapy techniques.* Cambridge: Harvard University Press.

Moffit, T., Caspi, A., Rutter, M., and Silva, P. 2001. *Sex differences in antisocial behavior.* Cambridge: Cambridge University Press.

Moeller, T. 2001. *Youth aggression and violence.* Mahwah, NJ: Erlbaum.

Morrison, G., Furlong, M., and Morrison, R. 1997. The safe school: Moving beyond crime prevention to school empowerment. In A. Goldstein and J. Conoley, eds., *School violence intervention: A practical handbook* (pp. 236–264). New York: Guilford.

Nasby, W., Hayden, B., and DePaulo, B. 1980. Attributional bias among aggressive boys to interpret unambiguous social stimuli as displays of hostility. *Journal of Abnormal Psychology, 89,* 459–468.

Nomaguchi, K., Milkie, M., and Bianchi, S. 2005. Time strains and psychological well-being: Do dual-earner mothers and fathers differ? *Journal of Family Issues, 26,* 756–792.

Office of Elementary and Secondary Education. 2002. Student-led crime prevention: A real resource with powerful promise. Washington DC: U.S. Department of Education, Safe and Drug-Free Schools Program.

O'Keefe, M. 1997. Adolescents' exposure to community and school violence: Prevalence and behavioral correlates. *Journal of Adolescent Health, 20,* 368–376.

Olweus, D. 1979. Stability of aggressive reaction patterns in males: A review. *Psychological Bulletin, 86,* 852–875.

Orobio de Castro, B., Veerman, J., Koops, W., Bosch, J., and Monshouwer, H. 2002. Hostile attribution of intent and aggressive behavior: A meta-analysis. *Child Development, 73,* 916–934.

Osher, D., Dwyer, K., and Jackson, S. 2004. *Safe, supportive, and successful schools step by step.* Longmont, CO: Sopris West.

Osofsky, J. 1995. The effects of exposure to violence on young children. *American Psychologist, 50,* 782–788.

Patterson, G., Reid, J., and Dishon, T. 1992. *Antisocial boys.* Eugene, OR: Castalia.

Pearce, J., and Pezzot-Pearce, T. 2007. *Psychotherapy of abused and neglected children.* 2nd ed. New York: Guilford.

Pittman, K., and Irby, M. 1996. *Preventing problems or promoting development?* Washington, DC: Forum for Youth Investment.

Prinzie, P., Onghena, P., and Hellinckx, W. 2006. A cohort-sequential multivariate latent growth curve analysis of normative CBCL aggressive and delinquent problem behavior: Associations with harsh discipline and gender. *International Journal of Behavioral Development, 30,* 444–459.

Putallaz, M., and Bierman, K. 2004. *Aggression, antisocial behavior, and violence among girls: A developmental perspective.* New York: Guilford.

Reid, J., Patterson, G., and Snyder, J. 2002. *Antisocial behavior in children and adolescents: A developmental analysis and model for intervention.* Washington, DC: American Psychological Association.

Repetti, R., Taylor, S., and Seeman T. 2002. Risky families: Family social environments and the mental and physical health of offspring. *Psychological Bulletin, 128,* 330–366.

Risi, S., Gerhardstein, R., and Kistner, J. 2003. Children's classroom peer relationships and subsequent educational outcomes. *Journal of Clinical Child and Adolescent Psychology, 32,* 351–361.

Rose, A., Swenson, L., and Waller, E. 2004. Overt and relational aggression and perceived popularity: Developmental differences in concurrent and prospective relations. *Developmental Psychology, 40,* 378–387.

Rose, L., and Gallup, A. 2003. The 35th annual Phi Delta Kappa / Gallup poll of the public's attitudes toward the public schools. *Phi Delta Kappan, 85,* 41–56.

Rubin, K., Bukowski, W., and Parker, J. 2006. Peer interactions, relationships, and groups. In N. Eisenberg, W. Damon, and R. Lerner, eds., *Handbook of child psychology,* vol. 3: *Social, emotional, and personality development,* 6th ed. (pp. 571–645). Hoboken, NJ: Wiley.

Rutter, M., Giller, H., and Hagell, A. 1998. *Antisocial behavior by young people.* Cambridge: Cambridge University Press.

Safran, S., and Oswald, K. 2003. Positive behavior supports: Can schools reshape disciplinary practices? *Exceptional Children, 69,* 361–373.

Sampson, R., Raudenbush, S., and Earls, F. 1997. Neighborhoods and violent crime: A multilevel study of collective efficacy. *Science, 277,* 918–924.

Sanders, M. 2003. Community involvement in schools: From concept to practice. *Education and Urban Society,* 35, 161–180.

Schaeffer, C., Petras, H., Ialongo, N., Poduska, J., and Kellam, S. 2003. Modeling growth in boys' aggressive behavior across elementary school: Links to later criminal involvement, conduct disorder, and antisocial personality disorder. *Developmental Psychology,* 39, 1020–1035.

Schwartz, D., and Proctor, L. 2000. Community violence exposure and children's social adjustment in the school peer group: The mediating roles of emotion regulation and social cognition. *Journal of Consulting and Clinical Psychology,* 68, 670–683.

Secret, M., and Peck-Heath, C. 2004. Maternal labor force participation and child well-being in public assistance families. *Journal of Family Issues,* 25, 520–541.

Shartrand, A., Kreider, H., and Erickson-Warfield, M. 1994. *Preparing teachers to involve parents. A national survey of teacher education programs.* Cambridge MA: Harvard Family Research Project.

Sherif, M. 2001. Superordinate goals in the reduction of intergroup conflict. In M. Hogg and D. Abrams, eds., *Intergroup relations: Essential readings—Key readings in social psychology* (pp. 64–70). New York: Psychology Press.

Shipley, P., and Coats, M. 1992. A community study of dual-role stress and coping in working mothers. *Work and Stress,* 6, 49–63.

Simmons, R. 2002. *Odd girl out: The hidden culture of aggression in girls.* New York: Harcourt.

Simons, R., Lin, K., Gordon, L., Brody, G., Murry, V., and Conger, R. 2002. Community differences in the association between parenting practices and child conduct problems. *Journal of Marriage and the Family,* 64, 331–345.

Snyder, H. 2006. Juvenile arrests, 2004. *Juvenile Justice Bulletin: Office of Juvenile Justice and Delinquency Prevention.* Retrieved February 20, 2007, from http://www.ncjrs.gov/pdffiles1/ojjdp/214563.pdf.

Snyder, J., Schrepferman, L., Oeser, J., Patterson, G., Stoolmiller, M., Johnson, K., and Snyder, A. 2005. Deviancy training and association with deviant peers in young children: Occurrence and contribution to early-onset conduct problems. *Development and Psychopathology,* 17, 397–413.

Snyder, H., and Sickmund, M. 1999. *Juvenile offenders and victims: 1999 national report.* Washington DC: Office of Juvenile Justice and Delinquency Prevention.

Sprague, J., and Walker, H. 2005. *Safe and healthy schools:Practical prevention strategies.* New York:Guilford.

Sprague, J., Walker, H., Golly, A., White, K., Myers, D., and Shannon, T. 2001. Translating research into effective practice: The effects of a universal staff and student intervention on indicators of discipline and school safety. *Education and Treatment of Children, 24,* 495–511.

Stahl, A., Finnegan, T., and Kang, W. 2003. Easy access to juvenile court statistics: 1985–2000. Online. Available at http://ojjdp.ncjrs.org/ojsta tbb/ezajcs/.

Stattin, H., and Kerr, M. 2000. Parental monitoring: A reinterpretation. *Child Development, 71,* 1072–1085.

Stattin, H., and Magnusson, D. 1989. The role of early aggressive behavior in the frequency, seriousness, and types of later crime. *Journal of Consulting and Clinical Psychology, 57,* 710–718.

Steinberg, M., and Dodge, K. 1983. Attributional bias in aggressive adolescent boys and girls. *Journal of Social and Clinical Psychology, 1,* 312–321.

Sugai, G., and Horner, R. 1999. Discipline and behavioral support: Practices, pitfalls, and promises. *Effective School Practices, 17,* 10–22.

Thomas, S., and Smith, H. 2004. School connectedness, anger behaviors, and relationships of violent and nonviolent American youth. *Perspectives in Psychiatric Care, 40,* 135–148.

Thorpe, G., and Olson, S. 1990. *Behavior therapy: Concepts, procedures, and applications.* Needham Heights, MA: Allyn and Bacon.

Tremblay, R., Pihl, R., Vitaro, F., and Dobkin, P. 1994. Predicting early onset of male antisocial behavior from preschool behavior. *Archives of General Psychiatry, 51,* 732–739.

Tucker, J., Petric, G., and Lindauer, P. 1998. Increasing order and safety on school buses. *ERS Spectrum, 16,* 27–32.

Underwood, M. 2002. Sticks and stones and social exclusion: Aggression among girls and boys. In P. Smith and C. Hart, eds., *Blackwell handbook of childhood social development* (pp. 533–548). Malden, MA: Blackwell.

U.S. Department of Health and Human Services. 2001. *Youth violence: A report of the surgeon general.* Washington DC: Government Printing Office.

Vail, K. 1997. Unruly cargo. *American School Board Journal, 184,* 34–36.

Vandell, D., Pierce, K., and Dadisman, K. 2005. Out-of-school settings as a developmental context for children and youth. *Advances in Child Development and Behavior, 33,* 43–77.

Vandell, D., and Wolfe, B. 2000. *Child care quality: Does it matter and does it need to be improved?* Washington DC: U.S. Department of Health and Human Services. Available at http://aspe.hhs.gov/hsp/ccquality00/index.htm.

Van Leeuwen, K., Mervielde, I., Braet, C., and Bosmans, G. 2004. Child personality and parental behavior as moderators of problem behavior: Variable- and person-centered approaches. *Developmental Psychology, 40,* 1028–1046.

Walker, S. 1999. Stemming the tide of youth violence. *Progress of Education Reform, 2,* 2–6.

Walker, S., Grantham-McGregor, S., Himes, J., Williams, S., and Duff, E. 1998. School performance in adolescent Jamaican girls: Associations with health, social and behavioural characteristics, and risk factors for dropout. *Journal of Adolescence, 21,* 109–122.

Walsh, W., Craik, K., and Price, R., eds. 2000. *Person-environment psychology: New directions and perspectives.* 2nd ed. Mahwah, NJ: Erlbaum.

Webster-Stratton, C. 1994. Advancing videotape parent training: A comparison study. *Journal of Consulting and Clinical Psychology, 62,* 583–593.

Weigel, D., Weigel, R., Berger, P., Cook, A., and Delcampo, R. 1995. Work-family conflict and the quality of family life: Specifying linking mechanisms. *Family and Consumer Sciences Research Journal, 24,* 5–28.

Weiner, B. 1986. *An attributional theory of motivation and emotion.* New York: Springer-Verlag.

——. 1992. *Human motivation: Metaphors, theories, and research.* Thousand Oaks, CA: Sage.

Wentzel, K. 1993. Does being good make the grade? Social behavior and academic competence in middle school. *Journal of Educational Psychology*, 85, 357–364.

Wentzel, K., and Asher, S. 1995. The academic lives of neglected, rejected, popular, and controversial children. *Child Development*, 66, 754–763.

Werner, N., and Crick, N. 2004. Maladaptive peer relationships and the development of relational and physical aggression during middle childhood. *Social Development*, 13, 495–514.

Whiting, B., and Edwards, C. 1988. *Children of different worlds: The formation of social behavior*. Cambridge: Harvard University Press.

Zahn-Waxler, C., and Polanichka, N. 2004. All things interpersonal: Socialization and female aggression. In M. Putallaz and K. Bierman, eds., *Aggression, antisocial behavior, and violence among girls: A developmental perspective* (pp. 48–68). New York: Guilford.

Index